KUALA LUMPUR

Segar
016 6113908

leg:

GW00497181

APA PUBLICATIONS

Part of the Langenscheidt Publishing Group

L

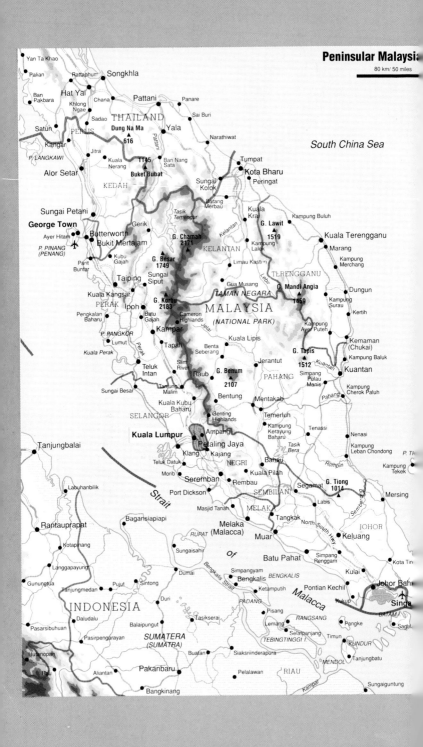

Welcome!

Less than 100 years ago, Kuala Lumpur was a run-down shanty-town sitting precariously on the edge of a marshy riverbank. But for some unfathomable reason, the people came – Malay farmers, Chinese merchants, British tin miners, Indian railroad workers – turning it into a cultural confluence with few parallels. Today, this former mining outpost has transformed itself into a bourgeoning city of two million, ready to meet the challenges of the next millenium.

In these pages, Shoba Devan, journalist, Insight correspondent and longtime resident of Kuala Lumpur has crafted itineraries perfect for a short stay. A selection of full- and half-day itineraries cover the city's must-see sights and optional extras. For those with time, there are longer excursions to lush rainforests, remote islands and even a Vegas-style casino on the outskirts of the city. Chapters on eating out, nightlife and shopping, plus a practical information section covering travel essentials complete this reader-friendly guide.

 Shoba Devan moved her base to Kuala Lumpur in 1982 out of sheer necessity. But as she became familiar with the city's smells, sounds and sights, she looked beyond the concrete skyscrapers and saw a certain rusticity about it. Despite its apparent modernity, the city has retained a certain idyllic charm. For Devan, the small-town hospitality manifests itself subtly – the smile of recognition from the neighbourhood soya bean milk hawker; the spirited political discussions of the local barber; and the hammy performances of sidewalk medicine men. Devan hopes this book will unleash the explorer in you and lead you to discover what really makes Kuala Lumpur tick.

C O N T E N T S

*Pages 2/3:
The ever-
changing Kuala
Lumpur skyline*

Excursions

These day-trips are designed to get you out of the city to experience rural Malaysia.

Pages 8/9: National Day parade

Nightlife, Eating Out & Shopping

Calendar of Events

Practical Information

Maps

Index and Credits 98–100

HISTORY & CULTURE

The Founding Of Kuala Lumpur

Kuala Lumpur was never the centre of an ancient culture or civilisation. No philosopher, scientist or general can lay claim to its inspiration. Indeed, just 100 years ago, it was nothing more than marsh, muck and mudbank.

In 1857, an expedition of Chinese tin miners headed up the Klang River from Peng Kalan Batu (now Port Klang), then the capital of the Sultanate of Selangor. They were prospecting for tin, a mineral that commanded the kind of attention that is reserved for oil these days. After several days, they arrived at the confluence of the Klang and Gombak rivers, where they had to stop as the rivers were too shallow to accommodate their fully-laden flotilla. Their resting place was nothing more than a tiny hamlet nestled in a quagmire of mud. Disgusted, the miners called the place Kuala Lumpur – literally meaning 'muddy confluence'.

Tin was eventually found in Ampang, upstream of Kuala Lumpur, but because the rivers were shallow, direct access to the mines was limited. Thus, Kuala Lumpur became a convenient staging point for supplies and ore to be brought in or sent out. Buoyed by high tin prices, Kuala Lumpur developed into a flour-

The imposing Sultan Abdul Samad building

ishing village by the 1860s. Chinese labourers were imported by the thousands to operate the mines that had opened up its hinterland. There were some Malays – mainly Bugis traders – but the Chinese immigrants began to dominate. Soon, Kuala Lumpur took on the veneer of a booming mining town – seedy brothels, gambling dens and organised crime. The aristocrats of Selangor at first did not interfere with this development.

They were content to collect export duties from the mined ore, and left the control of the Chinese immigrants largely in the hands of a community leader called the 'Kapitan China'. The most illustrious Kapitan was Yap Ah Loy. A Hakka immigrant who came to the country when he was only seventeen, Yap's tenure of office from 1868 till 1885 proved significant in the history of Kuala Lumpur.

Railway Station tower

Gradually, Kuala Lumpur's prominence grew. In 1867, Selangor was torn by civil war. The bone of contention was the right to collect export duties on tin. Initially, the war focused on gaining control of the forts sited at the river estuaries where the Malay royalty was based. The miners of Kuala Lumpur, fearing the war, shipped their ore through whatever river route was open to them. As duties from tin slowly dwindled in the ports, the warring parties moved into Kuala Lumpur.

Meanwhile, Yap Ah Loy allied himself with Tengku Kudin, the Viceroy of Selangor. His enemies were led by Syed Hashor, a determined and resourceful man who enlisted the help of other Malay chiefs and overran Kuala Lumpur in August 1872, razing it to the ground. In 1873, Tengku Kudin, with the help of Malay forces from Pahang, regained the town. Yap Ah Loy is credited with ensuring that Kuala Lumpur did not disappear back into the marsh. After the war, with the town ruined and tin prices low, the Chinese immigrants were ready to pack up and leave for greener pastures. Yap borrowed capital to redevelop Kuala Lumpur and cajoled the immigrants to inspire confidence. Five years later, the strategy paid off as tin prices soared. In 1879, for the first time, a British official was stationed in Kuala Lumpur. In 1880, Selangor moved its capital to Kuala Lumpur.

The next major personality in the city's history was Frank Swettenham, the Resident of Selangor appointed in 1882. Swettenham replaced the shanties and huts that formed much of Kuala Lumpur with brick structures. He was also responsible for the construction of the Kuala Lumpur–Klang railway link, ending dependence on the river.

The city continued to grow. An active policy of emigration, the setting aside of reserves, and the encouragement of agriculture on its periphery increased the Malay population while diminishing the economic stronghold of the Chinese migrants. Indian labourers were brought in to work on coffee and rubber estates and on the railroad. The city became more cosmopolitan.

In 1896, Kuala Lumpur was declared the capital of the Federated Malay States. Both world wars did little damage to the city, and in 1957, 100 years after the first mining expedition, the campsite was finally deemed worthy as the capital of sovereign Malaya. In 1963, Kuala Lumpur became the capital of Malaysia, and in 1972, it gained city status. Significantly, the city was also wrenched from Selangor and declared a Federal Territory, similar to the status enjoyed by Washington's District of Columbia. Since then the city has bloomed into one of the fastest growing in Southeast Asia. In some areas basic infrastructure has not kept pace with the city's unbridled growth. The traffic jams, pollution and crowded streets are evidence of this.

In recent years, Kuala Lumpur has been forging lofty tourist attractions in the form of glass and metal. The Petronas Twin Towers, whose identical towers blend Islamic concept with New York design, stand at 450m (1,471ft) and hold the current title for the world's tallest buildings. Not far behind is the 421m (1,377ft) Menara Kuala Lumpur, a telecom-and-tourism tower complete with a breathtakikng bird's-eye-view of the city.

A Melting Pot

Visitors to Kuala Lumpur will be fascinated by its obvious multiculturalism: there are Malays, Chinese, Indians, Eurasians, Portuguese and many people of mixed races. At one time, the city was divided along racial lines, with members of a race dominating an entire neighbourhood. These days, racially diverse neighbourhoods are more common.

Still, certain areas remain the stronghold of one dominant race. The Chinese occupy Chinatown of course, and much of the nearby Pudu, Sungai Besi and Salak South areas. They are mainly Cantonese, though a fair number of Hokkiens live there as well. Most are adher-

Deep in prayer at the Masjid Jamek

Early morning excercise at Merdeka Square

ents of the traditional Taoist and Buddhist faiths, though a substantial number have adopted Christianity.

The Malays have tended to congregate in the Kampung Bahru, Datuk Keramat, Ulu Kelang, Ampang and Sungai Pencala areas. Many still have *kampung* or village roots outside the city, but this is slowly changing. All are devout Muslims and the profusion of mosques, particularly in Malay neighbourhoods, attests to this.

The Indian neighbourhoods are mainly in the Jalan Tun Sambanthan and Sentul areas. Their presence here is related to the fact that Malayan Railways once maintained housing for their labourers in these areas. Most of the Indians were from South India, but a fair sprinkling of Northerners – notably Punjabis, Sindhis and Gujeratis – also came to Kuala Lumpur for business. Sri Lankan Tamils were also imported by the colonial authorities as administrative and clerical staff. Indians are mainly Hindu, though there is a very prominent Indian-Muslim community in Kuala Lumpur.

The kaleidoscopic nature of Kuala Lumpur society has given rise to a host of social and religious norms, some of which apply to only one community and others to all. It is traditional, for instance, to remove your shoes before entering the homes of Malays, Indians and Chinese. Pointing your foot at anybody is considered an insult by all three races. Among Malays, it is considered impolite to converse in a loud and raucous manner, but the Indians and Chinese are not too sensitive about this. The list goes on.

The religious practices of Muslims are central to their lives. Most pray five times a day and many offices have prayer rooms (*surau*). Eating with one's left hand is also considered inappropriate by both Muslims and Hindus. There are a number of books on handling culture shock in Kuala Lumpur. When in doubt, ask politely. Most KL-ites (as the people call themselves) are friendly and will not hesitate to help out visitors to their city.

Historical Highlights

1403 Malacca Sultanate begins when Parameswara flees from Sumatra to Malacca. Advent of Islam.

1857 Kuala Lumpur is founded by tin miners and becomes a staging point for the trading of tin. Chinese labour is imported by the thouands to operate the mines.

1867 Selangor is torn by civil war over the imposition of export duties on tin ore. The war spreads to Kuala Lumpur and in 1872, the city is razed to the ground.

1868–1885 Yap Ah Loy becomes 'Kapitan China' of Kuala Lumpur, develops the town and contributes significantly to the city's history during his tenure of office.

1882 Frank Swettenham is appointed Resident of Selangor, and continues its urban development. Swettenham is also responsible for the construction of the KL-Klang railway link. The Malay population increases due to the growth of agriculture and Indians are brought in to work on the railway, and coffee and rubber estates.

1895 Formation of the Federated Malay States.

1896 Kuala Lumpur is declared the capital of the Federated Malay States by the British.

1941–45 Japanese occupy the Malay Peninsula.

1945 Plans for a Malayan Union comprising the Federated and Unfederated Malay States and the Straits Settlements are unsuccessful.

1946 Rise of Malay nationalism. United Malays National Organisation (UMNO) is formed on March 1.

1948 Federation of Malaya is created. State of Emergency declared because of communist insurgency.

1951 The Malayan Chinese Association (MCA) forms a partnership with UMNO.

1953 The Malayan Indian Congress (MIC) joins the UMNO-MCA partnership, forming the tripartite Barisan Nasional (Alliance), which plays a major role in the country's independence struggle.

1955 In Malaya's first national election, the Alliance wins 80 percent of the votes cast.

1957 On August 31, Malaya becomes an independent nation, with Tunku Abdul Rahman as its first Prime Minister. Kuala Lumpur is made the capital of Malaya.

1961 Year-long state of Emergency declared over the communist threat.

1963 On September 16, Singapore, Sabah and Sarawak join Malaysia and Kuala Lumpur becomes the national capital.

1965 Singapore withdraws from Malaysia to become a republic.

1970 Tun Abdul Razak is Malaysia's second Prime Minister. New Economic Policy for economic restructuring introduced.

1972 Kuala Lumpur is accorded city status.

1974 Kuala Lumpur is annexed from Selangor to become the Federal Territory.

1975 Tun Hussein Onn takes over as Prime Minister.

1981 Datuk Seri Dr Mahathir Mohamad becomes Malaysia's fourth Prime Minister.

1986 The Proton Saga, the first locally manufactured automobile, rolls off the assembly line.

1991 The more liberal New Development Policy (Vision 2020) takes effect. It aims to make Malaysia a developed country by 2020.

1993 The first locally manufactured aircraft takes to the skies.

1996 Malaysia successfully launches its first satellite. The Kuala Lumpur Tower and the first stage of the Light Rail Transport (LRT) opens.

1997 Completion of the 450m-tall Petronas Twin Towers, the world's tallest buildings erected to date.

1998 Kuala Lumpur hosts the XVI Commonwealth Games in September. The economy takes a stumble and currency controls are imposed.

1999 The federal government's offices move to the new national administrative centre in Putrajaya.

Right, Petronas Twin Towers

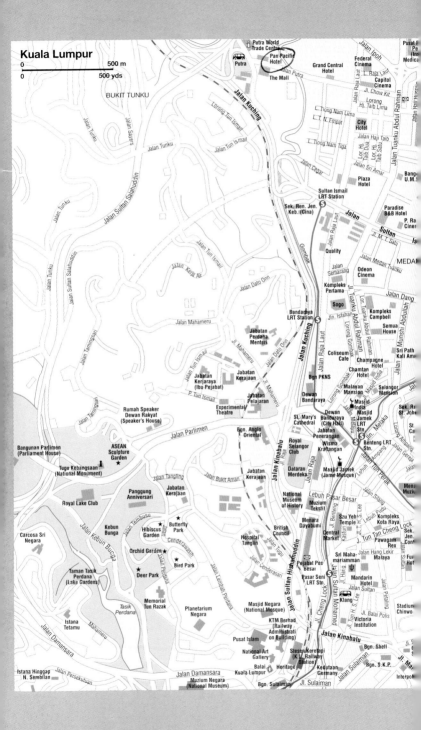

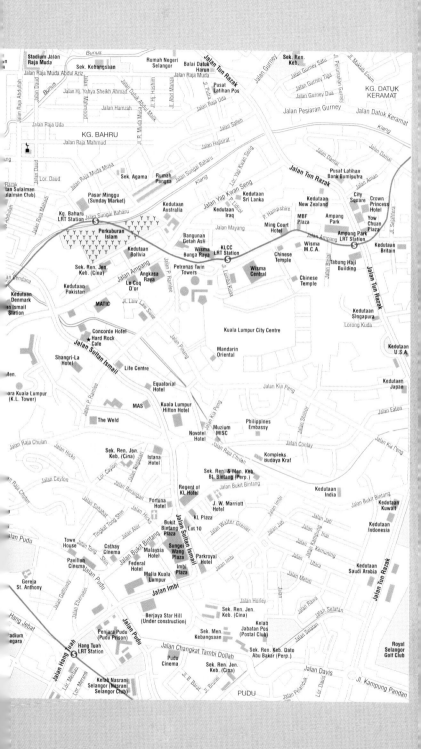

The first three days in Kuala Lumpur should be allocated to orienting yourself to this cosmopolitan city. The first day allows you to appreciate Kuala Lumpur's historic origins; the second, its present role as an exuberant marketplace; and the third, to reflect upon the quieter, greener areas of the city.

DAY 1

Getting Acquainted

Breakfast and a walk around Market Square; lunch at the stalls; historic hub; National Mosque; Railway Station and end the day with dinner at the Central Market.

This tour is designed to give you a feel of the city, from its origins as a colonial outpost to the thriving metropolis it is today. Start with a breakfast of steamed (yes, steamed) bread and *kaya* (a delicious jam of coconut and eggs) at the **Sin Seng Nam Restaurant** at **Medan Pasar Lama**. The square is one of the oldest parts of the

The Padang and Sultan Abdul Samad building

city, its Georgio-Romanesque facades resplendent, if somewhat incongruous with its surroundings, in the morning sun.

After breakfast, walk down the square towards the 12-storey Hong Kong Bank Building (opposite the Bank of Tokyo) and turn left. You are now at **Benteng**, and can clearly see the confluence of two rivers – the Gombak and Klang – that gives the city its name. Head along Benteng till you reach Jalan Tun Perak, then turn left and cross the bridge. In front of the Masjid Jamek LRT Station and on your left you will find the entrance to **Masjid Jamek** (Jame Mosque), a sprawl of spires that makes up the city's oldest mosque.

Further down, on the same side of the street, you will come to the city's most regal neighbourhood, despite the thrust of the LRT line. Done in Moorish majesty, these blocks of colonial buildings around the *Padang* (Green) have become representative of Kuala Lumpur. The building facing Jalan Tun Perak houses the **Sessions and Magistrates Courts**. Turn left at the junction with Jalan Raja and continue down past the bridge. Here, in the shade, petition writers hold sway. On the left is the former colonial administrative centre, the **Bangunan Sultan Abdul Samad**, now the Supreme Court.

Directly opposite is the Padang, fringed by a Tudor-style building on one side and a massive concrete plaza on the other. The cluster of wooden buildings is another colonial relic, the Dataran Merdeka Club, which prides itself on an ambience that dates back to the days when Somerset Maugham was a regular visitor.

Fountain at Dataran Merdeka

The national flag fluttering high

The massive plaza is the **Dataran Merdeka** (Independence Square), anchored by one of the world's tallest flagpoles and a giant video screen. Underground is a shopping arcade, theatre and restaurants.

Back across Jalan Raja is **Muzium Tekstil** (Textile Museum) (tel: 293 4858; daily 9.30am–6pm). This museum caters to textile enthusiasts, researchers and neophytes alike. Wander through the adjacent Museum Shoppe which carries various Malaysian paraphernalia, including textiles, woodcarvings and pottery.

For a quiet, relaxing lunch, try the hawker stalls behind the Muzium Tekstil, which offer a variety of spicy Malay meat and vegetable dishes to go with rice, making for decent budget meals.

Further down the same avenue is the gleaming white **Menara Dayabumi** (Dayabumi Complex), with its fine filigree-like Islamic design. It is at its most impressive at night when it is floodlit. Go

past the **General Post Office** (POS 2020) (Monday to Friday 7.30am–5pm, Saturday 7.30am–2pm, closed Sunday), and take the pedestrian subway to the other side of Jalan Sultan Hishamuddin. Ahead is the **Masjid Negara** or National Mosque (Saturday to Thursday 9am–6pm, Friday 3–6pm) with its 73m (240ft) tall minaret and geometric lattice-work. Resplendent in white marble offset by pools of gurgling water, the national mosque accommodates up to 10,000 people at a time. If you wish to enter the mosque, remove your shoes and use the robe provided if you are wearing shorts. Tour the interior to see the ornamental pools, fountains, a gallery, the library and the Grand Prayer Hall. Tourists, however, are forbidden from entering the Prayer Hall.

The last of the Moghul-style buildings to be constructed, the **Bangunan KTM Berhad** (Railway Administration Building), down the road from the mosque is architecturally stunning. Another Moorish extravagance, the **Stesen Keretapi Kuala Lumpur** (Kuala Lumpur Railway Station), stands opposite, and can be accessed by an underground pass beneath the busy road. The building is part of the city's proud efforts at architectural preservation. Built in 1885,

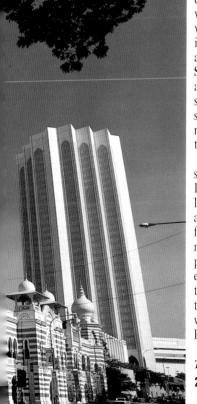

it was rebuilt at the turn of the century and extensively renovated in the 1980s and equipped with modern facilities, including tourist information kiosks and restaurants. The **Heritage Station Hotel** within it offers accommodation in an old-world setting. On the top floor of the station are backpackers accommodations – The Travellers Station – with nice views.

Walk through the railway station to get to Jalan Cheng Lock. From Platform 1, head left until you reach a subway and head for the exit on Platform 4. Occasionally, late at night, the famous and very expensive cream-and-white Eastern and Oriental Express (see the *Practical Information* chapter) train passes through on its way from either Singapore or Bangkok. The KTM Komuter

The Muzium Tekstil

Shop for souvenirs in Central Market

trains head out from Platforms 2, 2A and 3 to Port Klang, Seremban and Rawang.

You will now be facing **Jalan Cheng Lock**. Turn left and walk 500m (546yds) to the **Central Market (Pasar Seni)**. Once the city's largest wet market, this was converted in the late 1980s into a cultural-cum-shopping mall. Its art deco features and its high ceilings renovated and repainted recently, a great variety of goods are sold here, including handicrafts, souvenirs and art, all at fairly reasonable prices. Be sure to add an element of fun by bargaining for your purchases though. Regular evening cultural performances are held at the riverside amphitheatre. Pick up a brochure here or at the tourist office, and you may be lucky enough to catch a music, dance or shadow puppet performance

Jut outside, a pedestrian mall fronts quaint old shops selling dried fish, rice wine and porcelain Taoist icons. At the back is another row of pre-war shops turned souvenir shops and restaurants.

Head for the **Riverbank** (tel: 274 6652) at the Central Market for modestly priced Western and local dinner by the riverside, sometimes to live jazz.

Chinatown

Visit a money museum; walk down atmospheric Petaling Street; Chinese vegetarian lunch; visit Hindu and Chinese temples; and end the evening with an open-air seafood dinner.

Chinatown in Kuala Lumpur is similar to Chinatowns everywhere in the world (except perhaps China) – a colourful collage of earthy people, colourful temples and shops, and noisy restaurants.

Start the day by visiting a money museum, the **Muzium Numismatik**, or Numismatic Museum (daily 10am–6pm), located in the rear lobby of **Menara Maybank** (Malayan Banking Building) on Jalan Tun Perak. Once lording over Kuala Lumpur's skyscape, the building's fifty-one storeys have been dwarfed by the Kuala Lumpur and Petronas Towers.

Right across the roundabout in front of the money museum is Chinatown. Take the zebra crossing over to the Sinar Kota Shopping Complex. Ahead is one of the craziest traffic-choked roundabouts in the city, on the other side of which is the Puduraya Bus and Taxi Station – long-distance buses and taxis leave from here for destinations throughout the peninsula, Singapore and Thailand. At the top is the Puduraya Hotel, convenient for late night arrivals or early morning departures. At the roundabout, turn right into **Jalan Cheng Lock** and **Jalan Sultan**, which is the start of the Chinatown district.

Chinatown is concentrated in Jalan Petaling, Jalan Tun H S Lee and Jalan Hang Lekir. Interestingly, the character of Chinatown changes through the day. In the morning, people throng *dim sum* restaurants for breakfast and the wet market is active with housewives picking and prodding at the fresh produce. In the after-

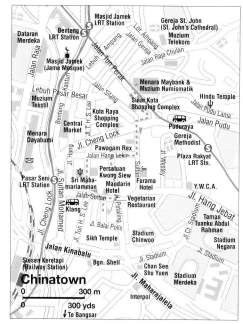

Chinatown

Mooncakes are sold only in September

noon, there is a lull, but come evening, numerous stalls selling food and merchandise are set up in preparation for the after-office hours crowd. For this reason, you may want to return to Chinatown in the evening to shop and eat, and enjoy the atmosphere.

Go down Jalan Sultan past the Rex Cinema and turn right into **Jalan Hang Lekir**, lined with shops selling dried pork floss and other Chinese delicacies. Stop at one of the many Chinese restaurants at the Petaling Street intersection and have a typical Chinese breakfast of *bak-kut-teh*, a fragrant stew of pork ribs and herbs, usually served from 6–10am. Like most food in Chinatown, this is not *halal* and therefore taboo for Muslims.

Just down the street, Jalan Hang Lekir meets Jalan Petaling. The latter is not just chaotic; it is pure anarchy. Here, sidewalk vendors and pedestrians compete with cars negotiating the narrow road. Shopping here is an exciting, even heady experience but some people find it demanding. Photographers need to ask before taking photos as many people object.

There are a couple of things you should know about shopping in Chinatown. First, to get the best price, bargain enthusiastically. Second, despite whatever you are told, it is not the place for designer labels. You may see vendors hawking Gucci handbags and Cartier watches which look uncannily like the real thing.

To get to your lunch spot, walk down Jalan Petaling towards Jalan Sultan. Turn right at Jalan Sultan and then left into a small alley called **Jalan Panggung** after 50m (165ft), just before the Ocean Supermarket. Walk down another 50m (165ft) and you will arrive at the **Wan Fo Yuan Vegetarian Restaurant** where you can

Striking contrasts of affluence and tradition at Jalan Sultan, Chinatown

Deity at Persatuan Kwong Siew Temple

try a reasonably-priced Chinese vegetarian meal. Chinese vegetarian cooking is an art form in its own right. The food is made to resemble meat or fish (and sometimes even tastes like the real McCoy) but is made entirely from soya bean gluten.

After lunch, turn right and head back towards Jalan Sultan, where you turn left and walk towards the junction with **Jalan Tun H S Lee**. Turn right at this junction and you will see the **Sri Mahamariamman Hindu Temple** (daily 8am–6pm) on the left side of the road. The temple is an arresting sight, all the more for its incongruent Chinese setting. Built in 1873, the temple occupies an important place in Hindu religious life, as it is from here that the annual Thaipusam pilgrimage to Batu Caves (see *Pick & Mix 3*) begins. Remove your footwear first if you decide to enter the Hindu temple. Outside, vendors sell fragrant jasmine flowers strung into garlands. Buy one, drape it around your neck, and let its fragrance revitalise you.

Further down on the right side of the road is the **Persatuan Kwong Siew Chinese Temple,** (open daily 7am–5pm) built by the Kwong Siew Association in 1888. Watch the devotees make incense offerings, continue your shopping spree, or return to your hotel if your legs don't feel up to it.

For dinner, take a taxi to **Bangsar Seafood Village** (tel: 282 2555) along Jalan Telawi Empat in Bangsar. The speciality here is Chinese-style seafood. Try the abalone with mushroom and shrimp, or ask the waiter about the catch of the day. The yam basket and sizzling tofu are also recommended. After dinner, walk around Bangsar, one of the city's more trendy areas with bars, pubs and shops.

Gateway to Sri Mahamariamman Temple

DAY 3

Lake Gardens and the National Museum

A Malay breakfast; morning stroll around Lake Gardens, visiting its deer, bird and butterfly parks, and hibiscus and orchid gardens; a spicy Indian lunch eaten off banana leaves; National Museum; dinner at an open-air hawker centre.

Alfred Venning, the former British State Treasurer, was more interested in the idea of creating a paradisiacal botanical garden amid lakes in the heart of Kuala Lumpur than with greenbacks. He succeeded eventually. Now, 100 years later, the name Venning scarcely means anything to KL-ites, but his legacy strikes deep in the heart of the city. The **Lake Gardens** (Taman Tasik Perdana), with its 104ha (257 acres) of close-cropped lawns, undulating hills and carefully cultivated gardens, is a sanctuary from the maddening mayhem of the city. The Lake Gardens are also a valuable green lung, helping to cleanse the city of its polluted air.

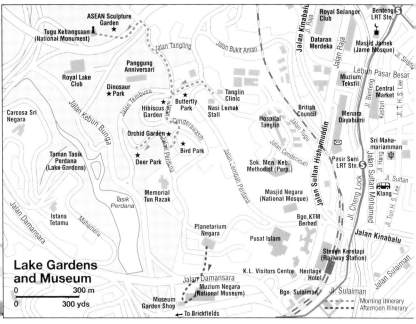

Lake Gardens and Museum

0 300 m
0 300 yds

Morning Itinerary
Afternoon Itinerary

Start the day early, with a breakfast of *nasi lemak* on the fringes of the Lake Gardens. Tell the taxi driver to take you to Jalan Cenderasi, on the left and off Jalan Sultan Hishamuddin after the National Mosque. Get off in front of the Tanglin Clinic. Directly opposite, under the shade of rain trees, is a stall selling *nasi lemak*, a typical Malaysian breakfast meal of fragrant rice cooked in coconut milk with side dishes like *ikan bilis sambal* (anchovies cooked with chillies), *rendang* (beef cooked with spices and coconut milk), peanuts and cucumber. Note that the stall is closed on Sunday.

Apart from the gardens, there are other attractions in the area, including the **Deer Park** with several local species, including the smallest species in the world, the mousedeer; **Bird Park**, one of the region's largest aviaries; **Butterfly Park**, a sanctuary for some 6,000 winged creatures; **Orchid Garden** and **Hibiscus Garden**, with hundreds of luxuriant blooms; and the quirky **Dinosaur Park**, where plants are pruned into dinosaur shapes.

You won't have time to visit all the parks in a few hours so take this suggested route. After breakfast, walk 200m (660ft) up the road to the **Butterfly Park** (daily 9am–6pm). Continue to the **Hibiscus**

Serenity at the Lake Gardens

27

An impressive salutation, the National Monument (Tugu Kebangsaan)

Garden (daily 9am–6pm), a 10-minute walk up Jalan Cenderawasih, where it meets Jalan Tembusu. Then follow the signs to the **Bird Park** (daily 9am–5pm) and the **Orchid Garden** (daily 9am–6pm). The nearby **Tun Razak's Memorial** is a tribute to Malaysia's second Prime Minister. Retrace your path to the **Deer Park** (daily 9am–6pm), which children especially seem to love. Instead of walking, you may prefer to use the park's shuttle bus, which operates daily from 9am–6.15pm with a break at lunchtime.

After a relaxing morning, backtrack to Jalan Cenderawasih and keep walking until you reach Jalan Parlimen. The **Tugu Kebangsaan** (National Monument) is just opposite Jalan Parlimen and contains fine sculptures and bronzework. The adjacent ASEAN **Sculpture Garden** features sculptures from the region (ASEAN is a regional economic and political association comprising Singapore, Malaysia, Indonesia, Brunei, the Philippines, Thailand, Myanmar, Laos, Cambodia and Vietnam).

As it will be lunchtime, take a taxi to **Brickfields**, just 2km (1¼ miles) or a 10-minute ride away. Try a typical South Indian lunch, eaten off a banana leaf, at the **Sri Devi Restaurant** on **Jalan Travers** (tel: 274 4173). Ask for either steamed plain rice, *beryani* (fragrant basmati rice), or *thosai* (rice flour-based pancakes). There

is a variety of side dishes to accompany the meal. Lentil gravy and vegetables come with the rice or *thosai,* and the spicy, dry-fried mutton is highly recommended. In true South Indian style, the meal is eaten with the fingers of the right hand only, but ask for cutlery

National Art Gallery

A National Museum mural

if you wish. Wash the meal down with a glass of cold *lassi*, a yoghurt-based drink. To end the meal, indulge in sweets like *jelebi*, *mysore pak* or *ladu*, but dieters be warned that these are made with loads of sugar and milk.

From Brickfields, take a cab to the **Muzium Negara** (National Museum; open daily 9am–6pm) where you can spend a couple of hours soaking up Malaysian history, especially its social and cultural sections; these include a section on the *Nonyas* and *Babas*, the unique fusion of Chinese and Malay traditions.

When you enter the main entrance, look out for the two huge Italian glass murals flanking it. The building itself is of interest, built in the old Malay *kampung* style with a huge Minangkabau-style roof. The museum features some offbeat exhibits – such as cats and treasures from dug-up graves, and the skull of an elephant which is said to have derailed a train in Malaysia – thanks to its former curator, Datuk Sharum Yub. The museum is small enough not to require a guided tour, so wander from room to room on your own. There is a charming **Museum Garden Shop** in the grounds, which is worth visiting for its local and Asian handicraft, including coconut-craft and ceramics.

A pedestrian bridge behind the museum leads to the **Planetarium Negara** (National Planetarium; tel: 273 5484; Saturday to Thursday 10am–4pm). However, if the gate is closed, there is a pathway across a little further down Jalan Damansara. The planetarium has a 14-inch telescope and a theatre. It also houses the Arianne IV space engine that was used to launch Malaysia's first satellite, the Measat I. Its well-designed garden is scattered with replicas of ancient observatories.

In the evening, go to **Jalan Alor** off Jalan Bukit Bintang for dinner (see *Pick and Mix 1*). By 6.30 or 7pm, food stalls line the entire street, selling all manner of local food. This is a great place to sample hawker fare from all over the country. The row of stalls at Penang Corner, diagonally across the Love Valley social escort service, offer specialities from Penang: *char kway teow* (broad, flat rice noodles fried with pork and bean sprouts), *mee yoke* (prawn noodles), *lobak* (mixed cold meats eaten with a chilly dip), *oh-luak* (fried oyster omelette) and *ikan panggang* (grilled fish). The *mee yoke* and *char kway teow* in particular are said to come close to the original stuff found in Penang.

After dinner stroll along **Jalan Bukit Bintang**, the road that never sleeps. These days, clubs and karaoke lounges provide the entertainment, but in the past, girlie bars and striptease shows were not uncommon. Still, if you search hard enough, you may find several 'escort agencies' operating from the dark alleys. Proceed entirely at your own risk.

The following half-day itineraries will take up five to six hours each to complete. These tours will open windows on Kuala Lumpur life, and whether you choose to do bustling Chinatown or the more sedate Kampung Bahru, the itineraries offer a microcosm of Malaysian life. Note that the hottest parts of the day are from 11am–4pm so keep in the shade, rest often and consume lots of liquids.

Morning Itineraries

1. Bukit Bintang

Kompleks Budaya Kraf; Maritime Museum, shopping; a leisurely stroll down Bukit Bintang before tucking into a wholesome Chinese porridge lunch.

This tour is a journey through Kuala Lumpur's most prestigious commercial and shopping area, 'the Golden Triangle'. And while a

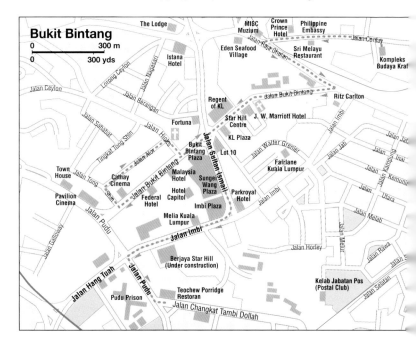

Busy street in Bukit Bintang

half-day is suggested, you may end up stretching it to a full day if you enjoy shopping. You can also use this tour to locate the shops you want to return to later.

Begin the morning at Jalan Conlay at the **Kompleks Budaya Kraf** (open daily 10am–6pm). This 'one-stop craft centre' showcases some of the best in Malaysian arts and crafts and houses commercial bazaars, a souvenir shop, a DIY batik corner, restaurant, Craft Museum, and an Artists' Colony.

Head up Jalan Conlay to Jalan Raja Chulan. On your left, amongst the trees you will see the **Seri Melayu Restaurant** (tel: 245 1833). You will also see **Eden Seafood Village** (tel: 241 4027) across the road. Both serve good Malaysian food with nightly entertainment. Just at the junction is the **Muzium MISC** (Monday–Friday 9am–4.15pm, Saturday 9am–12.15pm), devoted to maritime displays, is on the ground floor, with a good display of model boats, traditional craft, safety equipment and accounts of great maritime explorers. When finished, turn left and head to the **Jalan Bukit Bintang** intersection, where you should be extra careful when

Puppet figures from Malaysian folklore

Kites from Kelantan – a feast for the eyes

crossing the road. This is the beginning of Jalan Bukit Bintang, Kuala Lumpur's premier shopping area. Continue 500m (546yds) up the road until you see the **JW Marriott Hotel** and **Star Hill/CK Tang**'s on the left. Opposite is the **Regent of Kuala Lumpur**, with its classy decor, complete with live piano music in the foyer, considered one of the city's leading hotels. Star Hill houses CK Tang's, a Singapore-based department store, and exclusive designer boutiques.

Continuing on, you come to **Kuala Lumpur Plaza**, a four-storey shopping extravanganza, with the country's largest music store, the American chain **Tower Records**, as its anchor tenant. Right next to Kuala Lumpur Plaza is **Lot 10**, a fashionable hangout that has, in addition to upmarket shops and the Japanese-owned **Isetan Department Store**, numerous chic restaurants and coffee joints where the city's hip crowds like to hang out.

Across the street from the flashy Lot 10 is **Sungei Wang Plaza** (which you will visit later) and **Bukit Bintang Plaza**, both about 20m (65ft) left of the traffic lights and boasting large department stores. Sungei Wang's anchor tenant is **Parkson Grand**, while the upmarket **Metrojaya** dominates the Bukit Bintang Plaza. The real strength of these stores or, for that matter, most of the stores in this area, is clothing, from *haute couture* designer togs to the more moderately-priced Malaysian made apparel. To complement the clothing stores are innumerable shops selling shoes, belts, handbags, wallets and other leather accessories. Metrojaya, Tang's and Isetan

also have a good range of imported cosmetics and toiletries. Tip: even though cosmetics in Malaysia are duty free, prices at these stores are probably still lower than those found at so-called duty-free stores.

A Tourist Information Centre

Bukit Bintang's shopping delights do not stop at clothing. In all the malls mentioned, there are shops selling a whole lot of other goods, from watches and cameras to photographic equipment and books. The prices are reasonable as the area is popular with locals and competition among retailers is stiff. Sungei Wang, in particular, can get very crowded, especially during major festival periods. Most complexes feature cultural shows and music performances. To find out the programmes and schedules, check with the information desk that fronts each mall. Several times during the year, goods are marked down by as much as 70 percent.

From Bukit Bintang Plaza, turn left at the main entrance and head down Jalan Bukit Bintang. In stark contrast to the malls you have just seen (or shopped at) the stores that front the street are less exciting and do not offer the same range and quality of merchandise. In addition, cheap hotels, money changers, tour agents and karaoke bars line the street.

Keep walking and 500m (546yds) further down, you will come to the Federal Hotel. Then cross the road to the Cathay Cinema. Head down behind the cinema and you are in **Jalan Alor**. Keeping to the right side of the road, head down this street. Walk till you get to the top of the Jalan Hicks junction, turn right and you are back in Jalan Bukit Bintang.

If you find this part of Bukit Bintang quiet, rest assured it is only so during the day. When dusk falls, the area comes alive, and it is strongly recommended that you come back to sample its evening delights. Behind placid shop fronts and sanitised fast food outlets lurks another personality – one that comes out with the stars. The first sign of this is the bright neons and tell-tale red lights that seem to spring up from every second storey window. Jalan Alor metamorphoses from a congested city street into brightly lit chaos of food stalls selling a whole range of Chinese cuisine, from the mundane to the exotic – venison, tripe and seafood – for prices beginning at under RM5.

Night lights on Bukit Bintang

Cross the road and turn left until you reach a set of traffic lights. At the junction, turn right and head down **Jalan Sultan Ismail**. Keep to the right side of the road. At the traffic lights past Sungei Wang Plaza, turn right into Jalan Imbi. You will now be approaching **Imbi Plaza**, which backs Sungei Wang Plaza. Imbi Plaza is Kuala Lumpur's computer mall. You may want to look at the locally fabricated IBM clones on sale. Malaysia is the world's largest exporter of semi-conductor devices. A fully decked IBM clone, complete with colour monitor, costs around RM4,000.

Next door to Imbi Plaza is the **Melia Kuala Lumpur**. Here, you can get an aerial view of Kuala Lumpur if you ride the hotel's exterior bubble lift up to the 18th floor.

From the hotel, head down Jalan Imbi to get to **Jalan Pudu**. At the lights, turn left. On your right is **Pudu Prison**, built in 1895, and once housing the country's most notorious criminals. It is now awaiting re-development, although a small section might be retained as a museum. The mural on its wall makes up the world's longest painting. The **Teochew Porridge Restoran** (open daily 7am–3pm and 6pm–4am) at 270 Jalan Changkat Tambi Dollah, off Jalan Pudu (tel: 248 3452) specialises in, as the shops name says, Teochew porridge, a rice broth served with meat, fried fish and preserved vegetables. The restaurant also serves a very popular *dim sum*. After lunch, take a taxi to **Menara Kuala Lumpur** (daily 10am–10pm) to observe a vertigo-inducing view of the city from one of the world's tallest buildings.

2. Kampung Bahru Walk

A tour of the oldest Malay settlement; visit a Sikh temple and a mosque; and a browse through a Malay bazaar.

This tour takes you around the oldest Malay settlement in Kuala Lumpur – **Kampung Bahru** (founded in 1899), which is a real contrast to Chinatown. Although far more sedate, and less chaotic than Jalan Petaling, Kampung Bahru is still interesting, although

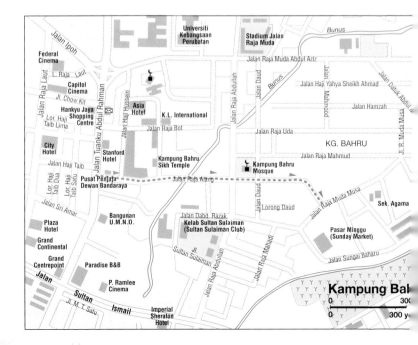

A Kampung Bahru fruit vendor

you will not find the variety of merchandise sold by Chinatown's sidewalk vendors.

Head down **Jalan Raja Alang** from its junction with **Jalan Tuanku Abdul Rahman**. The road is supposedly for vehicular traffic, but often the crowds spill over the sidewalks and onto the road. As you walk down Jalan Raja Alang, try some fruit from the stalls on the left. In addition to apples, oranges and bananas, some specialise in exotic tropical fruits that rarely see the light of a supermarket shelf. Depending on the season, you might find durians, mangosteens, rambutans, mangoes, papaya and pineapples, among others.

Further down, there is a municipal hawker food emporium, **Pusat Penjaja Dewan Bandaraya**, where Malay food is served. Try the *mee jawa* or *mee soup*, both noodle-based dishes, for breakfast, before continuing your journey.

One would have thought that a Sikh temple would be out of place in a largely Muslim neighbourhood, yet there it stands in its red brick glory to the left of the road, further down from the Pusat Penjaja food centre. The façade of the **Kampung Bahru Sikh Temple** is reminiscent of Kuala Lumpur's pre-war shophouses. The temple gates are normally closed to traffic, but there is a side entrance that allows individuals to enter. In consonance with the Sikh faith, there are no icons. Instead, pictures of Sikh saints line the entrance hall. The temple is open only occasionally and during special festivals, so you may have to make do with a view through the gates.

Head straight down Jalan Raja Alang till it meets Jalan Raja Abdullah. Just across the crossroads is the **Kampung Bahru Mosque**. Built around 1924, it was one of the first

The Kampung Bahru Sikh Temple

Kampung Bahru Mosque

concrete structures erected in the quarter. Indeed, the charm of Kampung Bahru lies in the architecture and layout of the houses. Typically made of wood, the houses are spacious and high-ceilinged, in keeping with Malay architectural tradition. Often, prayer mats or religious writing grace the door, underscoring the intense devotion many Muslims have for their religion.

Houses like these line the stretch of Jalan Raja Alang beyond the mosque, though much has been sacrificed to the efficiency of modern office block structures. The residents do not normally open their homes to the public, but on the rare occasion, it may be possible to gain privileged entry, depending on the predisposition of the occupants.

Songkoks – Muslim religious headgear

The road ends in a row of shophouses and a mini-bazaar. Here, you can indulge in more local cooking and the variety is really breathtaking.

From here, you can hail a taxi back to your hotel or to the ultra-modern Suria KLCC at the base of the **Petronas Twin Towers** on Jalan Ampang. The shopping centre has shops aplenty, cinemas, food outlets, an art gallery and a park. You might want to end your day at a performance in the concert theatre.

Note: During the fasting month of Ramadan, do this tour in the evening instead, just before the break of fast at sunset when the streets are a riot of stalls, and you can sample food cooked only during this period.

3. Batu Caves

A challenging walk up to a limestone cave temple filled with Hindu deities and mythological art.

This one is sure to awaken your calf muscles. No visit to Kuala Lumpur is complete without a trip to the caves, one of the holiest Hindu shrines, an intrigue for cave ecologists and geologists, and a popular tourist attraction.

The caves are popular for many reasons. Not only is it the southern-most limestone outcrop in the Northern Hemisphere, the labyrinth that makes up **Batu Caves** (open daily 7am–7pm) also supports a variety of exotic wildlife. The main cave holds a shrine of Lord Subramaniam, a deity revered by the Hindus. Every year,

Interior of the Batu Caves

at a festival called Thaipusam, hundreds of thousands of devotees, watched by a fair share of the curious converge at the shrine, offering thanksgiving and some undergoing self-flagellation, such as piercing their bodies with sharp spokes, as a sign of their devotion.

For centuries, the caves were obscured by thick jungle, and known only to forest inhabitants living nearby. In 1878, the caves were discovered by American naturalist William Hornaday. The existence of the caves soon became known to the public and the caves became a popular picnic spot for the colonial masters and their wives. During the Japanese occupation, Batu Caves served as a hideout for anti-Japanese communist guerilla forces. It was only years later that the local Hindu population, with their predilection for sacred caves, began making pilgrimages here to celebrate the Thaipusam festival.

Getting to Batu Caves is not a problem as lots of city taxis service the area. The first thing you will notice as you approach the main gates is the immense concrete staircase that leads up to the temple caves. There are 272 steps in all, making it quite a climb. Monkeys perch in perfect nonchalance along the staircase, and will quite will-

Mythology thrives in the Gallery of Indian Art

ingly accept bananas (or for that matter, just about anything else) in mock humility. You can buy fruits and nuts to feed the monkeys at food stalls near the row of shops to the right of the staircase. These monkeys are not tame enough to touch though, and a comfortable distance is well advised.

Once inside the main cave, take care to observe religious sensitivities by respecting those praying and keeping a distance from the shrines. Climb down the steps and once back on *terra firma*, you may want to visit the **Gallery of Indian Art**, located to the left of the staircase. Set in another cave, it features clay figurines from Indian mythological tales. True to the art form, the sculptures of Indian deities and scenes from Indian mythology are painted with bright, sometimes verging on the garish, colours.

There are a couple of souvenir shops, but besides the 'I was at Batu Caves' pendants, there is nothing you cannot get in the city. One shop specialises in fresh coconut water served in the nut itself. The others serve mainly Indian food at very reasonable prices. One shop specialises in Indian religious paraphernalia such as oil lamps, camphor holders, incense holders and icons. Depending on your taste, this shop can be a collector's paradise.

If you don't like crowds, avoid visiting at weekends, holidays and Thaipusam, when it's almost impossible to move.

4. Agriculture Park

See a nutshell of Malaysian agricultural activities and visit the Blue Mosque in Shah Alam. Bring a packed meal and drinks for the day; fishing enthusiasts should also bring their own gear.

This tour is definitely for those who enjoy nature. Located some 30km (19 miles) from Kuala Lumpur, the **Taman Pertanian Malaysia** (Malaysia Agriculture Park; tel: 550 6922; daily 9am–5pm) is a showcase of Malaysian agriculture. Carved from

Map of the Agriculture Park

1,295 ha (3,200 acres) of tropical forest in Bukit Cahaya Seri Alam, Shah Alam, the park features many facets of agriculture, livestock and fisheries in rustic surroundings. To get there by bus, take the Intrakota 338 or Cityliner 222 from the **Klang Bus Station** at Jalan Sultan Mohamed.

The entrance to the park includes the cost of a bus shuttle service. Alternatively, you may want to rent bicycles, which apart from letting you cover more ground, is a great way to exercise. From the gate, it is only a short walk to the park administration building where you can collect literature and maps on present and planned facilities. Maps are also clearly displayed at all shuttle bus shelters in the park.

A highlight of the park is the **Tropical Fruit Garden,** which has been planted with exotic species such as durian, mangosteen and rambutan trees. If you visit outside of the fruit season, you may have to be satisfied with a canopy of dense boughs and dried branches. Another interesting feature is the paddy field and rice milling plant. They are models of paddy fields that dominate the countrysides of many Asian countries.

Climb the hill behind the milling plant and walk through the cocoa estate to the fisheries lake. Here, in pleasant surroundings, you can fish to your heart's content in the company of fellow anglers. However, you have to bring your own gear. Even if you don't plan to fish, visit the boat-shaped fisheries centre, which features various facets of the local fishing industry.

There are numerous other attractions: the animal park, aviary,

A model rice field at the Agriculture Park

Landscaped gardens in Agriculture Park

fish cages, spice garden, orchid and flower gardens, temperate garden, mushroom garden, and cultural village, but they are a good hike or ride away and would take up most of the day. Just follow the maps at the bus shelters, or those you might have collected at the administration building. Clearly defined trails lead through the forest to isolated destinations like **Sapu Tangan Hill**. If this appeals to you, then along the way, you might also like to visit the Air Kuning and Sungai Baru lakes.

Air Kuning Lake is in the middle of a tropical forest. There are many good fishing spots but many come just for the relaxing atmosphere. Photographers especially will find many opportunities for great outdoor shots. If you want to trek and enjoy the natural environment, there are numerous hiking trails that meander through the forest, all of which are clearly marked. **Sungai Baru Lake** features a 'cage culture' complex where fish varieties like the *tilapia*, river catfish, sultan fish and other exotics, are reared in floating cages. There is no charge for entering the cage complex area.

The park also has a hydroponics garden and aviary. Within the park, chalet-style accommodation (tel: 550 7048 for reservations) designed to mimic life in a traditional Malay kampong, is also available.

There are a number of stalls at the park serving drinks and food. Some of the more isolated stalls only open during weekends and holidays. However, the canteen near the rice garden is usually open.

On the return trip, stop at the Selangor state mosque, the **Masjid Salahuddin Abdul Aziz Shah (Blue Mosque)**. Its blue dome is one of the most prominent structures in the city – in fact, the dome is bigger than that of St Paul's in London. The mosque is laid out along the same lines as the Great Mosque of Mecca and much of the design is influenced by contemporary Arabic architecture. When entering the prayer hall, you will notice that the mosque's 'ceiling fans' do not hang down from the ceiling at all, instead they are mounted on stalks from the ground.

Mushroom culture

Standing proudly before the Sultan Salahuddin Mosque, Shah Alam

The mosque grounds have been extensively landscaped with gardens and a pool which links up to the Shah Alam lake gardens, popular with locals. Before touring the interior of the mosque, remember to remove your footwear, ensure that you are appropriately dressed and that it is not the Muslim prayer time.

After this, it is time to head back to the city. If you had negotiated with the taxi driver for a return trip earlier, ask to be sent directly to your hotel.

5. The National Zoo and Aquarium

Visit the national zoo to see endangered animal species; the national aquarium; and a Malay hawker fare lunch.

While Kuala Lumpur's zoological gardens cannot compare with San Diego's or Singapore's, they do give an insight into the rich wildlife found in Malaysia. Both the zoo and the national aquarium are located on the same grounds and you can see both for the price of one entry ticket. Take the KTM Komuter to the Setapak Jaya Station and hail a taxi from there to **Zoo Negara** (National Zoo; daily 9am–6pm), located some 13km (8 miles) away from the city centre. Getting a taxi back to town is also not a problem although traffic jams on Jalan Ampang can be.

At one time, the zoo was set amidst virgin jungle and rubber estates. The urban sprawl, however, has caught up with the 25-ha (62-acre) zoo, and today it stands like an oasis in the midst of a concrete jungle. In all, there are about 400 species of Malaysian and exotic mammals, reptiles and birds on display.

From the zoo's entry gate, numerous paths meander between wooded groves and tree-lined enclaves where the animal enclosures

Taking a rest after lunch at the zoo

are located. Among the more exotic exhibits are the Sumatran tiger, Malayan tapir, orang utan and gibbons (the least evolved of all the apes). All are on the endangered list and are extremely rare outside this part of the world. Other attractions include the Malayan honey bear and the world's smallest deer, the mousedeer. In addition to these, you will find birds, monkeys, wild buffalo, giraffes, lions, camels and elephants.

The **Tunku Abdul Rahman Aquarium** is located at the back of the zoo and also boasts some unusual specimens, such as the Malayan Bony Tongue, Malaysian riverine carps and coral reef fishes. The aquarium displays over 80 species of aquatic animals, both freshwater and marine.

While there is a reasonable amount of shade, it can still get quite hot. If you are not up to walking, the zoo provides a shuttle bus that covers most of the exhibits. Still, for those hot and thirsty, there are numerous vending machines dispensing canned and packet drinks throughout the grounds of the zoo.

For food, there is only a Kentucky Fried Chicken outlet, though a small kisok dishing out local fare and a couple of stands that serve ice cream and other snacks are also an option. If you fancy something local, stroll beyond the car park. Adjoining the main road is a row of food stalls serving Malay food. Besides the good food, this is also an ideal place to hail a cab back to your hotel.

Afternoon Itineraries

6. Chow Kit

Shopping at The Mall and an early dinner at Medan Hang Tuah; a walk down Chow Kit; and an open-air bazaar.

Mention **Chow Kit** to any KL-ite and watch the sly grins spreading over their faces. There is a good reason for it, Chow Kit was once the most notorious neighbourhood in the city. Today, urban renewal has sanitised much of what was once KL's sleaze centre. But old impressions die hard. Besides, such things are not easily suppressed. In the backlanes and dark alleys of a Chow Kit evening, transvestites still ply their trade and call girls stare from behind masks of cheap make-up. It does not come close to Bangkok's Patpong Road, but is exciting enough for Kuala Lumpur.

Chow Kit is home to a chic shopping plaza, **The Mall**, at the end of **Jalan Putra**. Begin your walk from here. The Mall is resplendent in shining glass and concrete, and houses a host of upmarket establishments, including the Japanese retail chain, **Yaohan**. Adjoining The Mall is the **Legend Hotel**. Taking up almost half of the fourth floor is a food court called **Medan Hang Tuah**. Modelled on Kuala Lumpur in the 1930s, doorways, street lights and building facades of the period have been painstakingly re-created. The food court offers an immense variety of Malay and Chinese food. Have an early dinner here.

After checking out The Mall, head down Jalan Putra towards **Jalan Chow Kit**, about a 15-minute walk, or a short taxi ride away. Continue past the cross roads to **Jalan Tuanku Abdul Rahman**. This point marks the beginning of the Chow Kit shopping

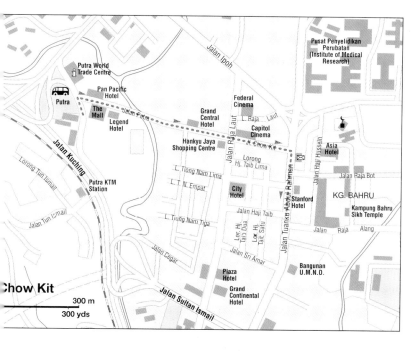

The Mall – for chic shopping

zone, a bazaar so elaborate that only major landmarks are given.

Start on the side of the road you are now on and walk in the direction of the traffic. All the stores lining the street have cheap goods but don't forget to bargain. The sidewalk, in the meantime, becomes noticeably crowded, as vendors open up stalls that sell what seems like everything under the sun. It gets even better on the opposite stretch. Continue walking down the road and use the crossing to get to the other side. The bazaar here occupies (though 'congests' is a better word) not only the sidewalks of Jalan Tuanku Abdul Rahman, but the side streets as well. This is the place for one of the most colourful and lively night markets. The authorities have long since given up on ensuring vehicular traffic flow, and pedestrians have taken over. Buses fly down this road with horns blaring; don't get in their path!

The range of goods is extensive, but as in Chinatown, do not be deceived by fake designer labels and brands. Prices are inflated so don't be shy of bargaining – in fact, be absolutely ruthless; it is not unusual to get discounts of at least 20 percent. When you get peckish, there is lots of street food for sale.

Shops galore at the Mall

Lunch at the Coliseum Cafe; wander down Jalan Tuanku Abdul Rahman and explore the Masjid India area; visit Little India and enjoy a North Indian dinner.

Built in 1928, the **Coliseum Cafe and Hotel** located next to the Coliseum Cinema on Jalan Tuanku Abdul Rahman has definitely seen better days. Its original decor, mismatched furniture and fittings disguise a once popular drinking hole for prosperous colonial planters, tin miners and traders. It still serves good, hearty meals and the waiters in their white jackets make for an entertaining (and reasonably-priced) meal. The sizzling steaks are recommended. Start your tour with lunch here.

A relic of early Kuala Lumpur, the cafe's facade has been maintained and provides sharp contrast to nearby fast food outlets. Notice how the cafe blends the antiquity of the city with 20th-century slickness. Upstairs are modest guest rooms at reasonable rates.

After lunch, join the hundreds on the pavements of **Jalan Tuanku Abdul Rahman**, the city's longest shopping street and named after the first king of independent Malaysia. To the locals, however, this area is popularly known as Batu Road. Merchandise ranging from textiles and carpets to shoes and leather goods are hawked by both shop and sidewalk vendors. There are also many *kedai makan* or eating shops, some of whose food should definitely be sampled.

To thoroughly enjoy this street, head down left from the Coliseum Cafe along the sidewalk. One of the first shops you come to is **Minerva Bookstore**, specialising in Islamic literature. English titles are also available. They have another store on the opposite side of the road. Further on, **Central Shoe Store** has one of largest range of footwear in the city. Other stores sell a variety of goods from sporting gear to textiles. **Sogo Department Store** on your left is a gigantic Japanese outlet with a supermarket, bookshop, restaurants, and a slew of luxury and bargain goods. Its

periodic sales are good value.

You are now at the junction of Jalan Tuanku Abdul Rahman and Jalan Dang Wangi. Cross the street and backtrack along the opposite side. Shoppers will experience a bizarre feeling of tranquillity on this road, espite the bustling atmosphere. With its mix of new shopping malls and established older stores, this strip offers an eclectic blend of consumer options. **Peiping Lace** and the **China Arts Co** at No 217 and 223 are two Chinese-run stores that are worth visiting. The stores sell quality antiques.

One of the country's oldest department stores, **Globe Silk Store**, located further down, offers some of the cheapest clothing buys in the city. Globe prides itself on its low prices and high quality, a tradition it has maintained for almost 60 years. There are five floors of clothing including batik shirts and the Malay *baju kurung* ladieswear, textiles, cosmetics and carpets in the Globe, while the top floor has a very nice cafeteria. You may want to take a break with a cold drink and curry puff (pastry stuffed with curried vegetables and meat) here.

Further down the street, at 135 Jalan Tuanku Abdul Rahman, the **P Lal Store** has earned itself a reputation with discerning

Fabrics of all colours and designs

shoppers. The smaller **Chotirmall Store** is also worth looking in. There are several textile stores along the way where fabrics and garments from all over Asia are sold. Although prices are generally fixed in the larger department stores, it is possible to bargain at the smaller shops. Some visitors enjoy this, they feel it adds to the shopping experience.

Yet further down the road more restaurants and textile stores are located within the 'five foot way', the local term for a shaded footpath. There are a few shops selling costume jewellery, hair bands and other accessories. The prices vary according to the material and quality, but be prepared to bargain. On Saturday evenings, the street is turned into a pedestrian mall and a night market sprouts up along the entire stretch. Like all night markets in Malaysia, the prices are low and the variety is staggering. Vendors sell everything, from fresh meat and vegetables to clothes and household items. Try not to miss this night bazaar – the atmosphere alone is worth experiencing.

As you continue down the street, you will first meet the junction with Jalan Melayu, then the major intersection with Jalan Tun Perak and the overhead LRT track. Turn left into Jalan Tun Perak. The Moorish structure across the road was built during the colonial days and now accommodates courthouses.

As you walk down Jalan Tun Perak, you will pass on the left the Bank of Commerce building before coming to Jalan Melayu and the Masjid Jamek LRT Station (opposite its namesake, the Jame Mosque). Turn into Jalan Melayu. Across the road, the Klang River is undergoing a major clean-up.

On your left are a row of shops that specialise in Indian *sarees* and fabrics. Among them are restaurants that dish up Indian breads and curries. Whether the heat is getting to you or not, this is an excellent opportunity to try a cold yoghurt-based drink called *lassi*. Opt for the sweetened or fruit-

Jalan Tuanku Abdul Rahman

.d version. There is a range of Indian desserts on sale, including diabetes-inducing red-orange sweet called *jelabi*, and *gulab jamun*, a round milk fritter soaked in syrup.

Head out of your restaurant and cross the road into **Jalan Masjid India**, an area of marked Indian-Muslim accent. Every available space on Jalan Masjid India, which runs parallel to Jalan Tuanku Abdul Rahman, is taken up by shops, restaurants and a colourful blend of sidewalk stalls. Among them are artists, and the ubiquitous sidewalk medicine seller whose concoctions can allegedly cure any ailment from snake bites to sexual maladies. For pure theatrical appeal, it is hard to beat the style of these street peddlers; a sure crowd-puller with their fast-paced narration of unbelievable medicinal wonders. Despite language barriers, it's possible to get a general idea of what they're touting.

Jalan Masjid India begins, ironically, with a cluster of Malay

shops (Wisma Yakin) on your right. The shops sell clothes and food, but one interesting shop specialises in *jamu*, a traditional cure-all medicine made from grounded herbs. Many Malays swear by this stuff, which reportedly also works wonders for the libido. On the left is **Masjid India**, an Indian-Muslim mosque after which the

Medicine man at Jalan Masjid India

street is named. Although it is only open to Muslim worshippers, do stop to appreciate its typically Indian-Muslim architecture, with tall spires reminiscent of the Taj Mahal.

Immediately left of the mosque is a stretch of shops housed within the **Malayan Mansion**. The seven-storey, yellow-orange

A Muslim faithful in front of the Indian Muslim mosque

Sarees and knick-knacks for sale in Little India

building is one of the oldest in the area. The first two levels are crammed with establishments that trade an enormous variety of merchandise. Diagonally opposite is the **Selangor Mansion**, also similarly jammed. Almost anything can be bought in the two mansions, but the area is better known for its speciality shops dealing in Indian textiles, Indian ethnic music tapes, religious icons, brassware and other exotica.

As you stroll down the road, buy a cooling drink of *mata kuching* (longan tea) or coconut juice from one of the many drink vendors. Along the way too are public toilets indicated by the signs saying *tandas*. The road branches into a fork in front of the Selangor Mansion; the narrower street on the right is **Medan Bunus**. The broad divider explodes in a blaze of colour with buckets of freshly-cut blooms and religious garlands displayed on wire enclosures. The flower-sellers here will thread the blossoms any way you want, from simple hair adornments to lavish bridal car arrangements.

Back onto Masjid India, the shops continue down the street. On your left is **Car and Company**, one of the country's oldest and best known sporting goods stores. Nearby are the budget accommodation-styled Chamtan, Palace and Empire hotels. They are popular with foreign backpackers, not surprising given their colourful ambience, central location and access to cheap, good food. At the end of the street are more shops, including money changers, a pharmacy and clothing stores. Indian cutlery stores along this row specialise in Indian stainless steel cutlery.

Masjid India terminates when you see a shopping mall called **Semua House**. There are a few shops here that sell costume jewellery, clothes, video cassettes and other merchan-

Indian plastic bracelets

49

dise. Exit left from Semua House, walk past City One Plaza, turn right at the end of the street and walk through the carpark. From here, be careful not to miss the tiny, almost kitschy, Hindu temple en route. Leave the temple, go left and return to Jalan Masjid India. Retrace your steps back to Jalan Tun Perak and the Masjid Jamek LRT Station. Turn left and walk towards the traffic lights at Lebuh Ampang.

On the left, just before the traffic lights, is the Majid Jamek LRT station, with a monstrous McDonald's beside it. Turn left into Lebuh Ampang and continue into Little India. The area still has a distinctly Indian feel; try a bag of mixed spicy Indian munchies. Several shops deal in Indian-style filigree 22-karat gold. Indian jewellery is traditionally chunkier and more ornate than Western gold jewellery. There are also some old-time money lenders, *saree* shops and Indian vegetarian restaurants. Store-owners are quite willing to bargain, so take time to peruse the melange of goods.

Continue to the end of the street and turn right into Jalan Gereja, past St John's Cathedral and Jalan Bukit Nanas which goes to Kuala Lumpur's last natural forested area, the **Bukit Nanas Recreational Park**, which has a pathway to the Kuala Lumpur Tower. At the junction of Jalan Raja Chulan is the restored neo-classical **Muzium Telekom** (tel: 201 9966, Monday–Friday 8.30am–4.45pm, Saturday 8.30am–1pm), which charts Malaysia's telecommunications history. The 1928 building used to house a pre-war manual telephone exchange.

Return to your hotel, freshen up for dinner and catch a taxi to **Bangles** restaurant on **Jalan Tuanku Abdul Rahman**. This restaurant serves good North Indian dishes such as *tandoori* and *kebabs*, accompanied by slabs of a hot oven-baked bread called *naan*. Wash the meal down with spicy Indian *masala* tea.

A sidewalk biscuit vendor

8. Klang Valley

A trip to the richest and fastest-growing area in Malaysia, followed by a seafood dinner in the port.

This bus or train tour takes you down the **Klang Valley**, the most dynamic, wealthiest and industrialised region in the country. The route is roughly parallel to the Klang River. Just 130 years ago, miners led a prospecting expedition up the same river in search of tin and ended up founding Malaysia's capital city, Kuala Lumpur. The Klang Valley then was totally inhospitable with impenetrable jungle and swamp. Much of this has disappeared with urbanisation.

Klang bus station

Kuala Lumpur's first link with the outside world was via a railway line built by Sir Frank Swettenham in 1886. Today, sleek, electric commuter trains service the route spanning Port Klang to Rawang in the north. Regular services leave Kuala Lumpur Railway Station, Platform 2A, for **Pelabuhan Klang (Port Klang)** and it is preferable to catch the train for at least one leg of this trip.

Start with an early lunch of *yong tau foo* (stuffed tofu and vegetables) at the stall along **Jalan Thambapillay** at the T-junction with Jalan Tun Sambanthan in Brickfields. For drinks, a nearby stall sells sugar cane juice and coconut water.

After lunch, take a taxi to the **Klang Bus Station**. The express bus services to Klang are easily located and are operated by the Klang Banting Express line. Comfortable, air-conditioned buses leave every half hour or so. Just board a bus and wait for the conductor to approach you for the fare. The first area the bus passes is the massive railroad yard at Brickfields, near where you lunched earlier. A century ago, the kilns of Brickfields supplied all the requirements of a rapidly growing town. The name still sticks despite the fact that the kilns were relocated long ago. A central transport terminal is being built here.

The bus passes through **Jalan Bangsar**, then swings onto the eight-lane Federal Highway, the main road link to Klang. Just after entering the highway, you pass under an archway that signals the division between the restless urban sprawl of Kuala Lumpur

Crest at Sultan Sulaiman Mosque

and its less frenzied satellite town, **Petaling Jaya**.

Petaling Jaya, sensibly abbreviated to PJ, was developed originally as a low cost housing scheme in the late 1950s. It has since blossomed into a middle-class area of over 500,000 inhabitants who incidentally have the highest rate of personal car ownership in Southeast Asia. After PJ, the bus goes past **Sungai Way**, a suburb of PJ (when a satellite town begins to have its own suburb, you know it has arrived) where most of the electronic factories are located. PJ merges into another middle-class suburb, **Subang Jaya**.

The bus then enters **Shah Alam**, the capital of the state of Selangor, which was hewn in the 1970s out of rubber plantations, and is one of the country's best planned cities with broad boulevards and huge roundabouts. The highway traverses the town, dividing it into two distinct sections: on the left its industrial face, already larger than that of PJ and still growing; and on the right its residential enclave.

Within the High Technology Park on the left, though not visible from the bus, is the Perusahaan Otomobil Nasional (Proton) factory, Malaysia's first national car manufacturer, whose products dominate the roads. Further, on the right is the towering spire and distinctive powder-blue dome of the **Masjid Sultan Salahuddin Abdul Aziz Shah (Blue Mosque)**. Next to the mosque, the skyline is dominated by the office towers of downtown Shah Alam.

While there is little semblance of a green belt between Shah Alam and Klang, the distinction between the two towns is marked. Klang is old, in fact, older than Kuala Lumpur. The streets meander between pre-World War II shops, houses and overgrown rain trees. About 10km (6 miles) to the west is **Pelabuhan Klang** (Port Klang), Malaysia's biggest and busiest port, but the town after which it is named seems totally unaffected.

In contrast, **Klang's** bus station is bedlam, located in that part of the town centre where

Sultan Sulaiman Mosque

most of the larger supermarkets and department stores operate. As you exit the bus depot you will notice a taxi stand in front of the largest department store. The train station is not well serviced by taxis, but wait patiently. There are no tour bus facilities operational in Klang, so you would have to hire a taxi for the trip. The rate varies according to the time the taxi is hired, but generally it is about RM15 per hour. Agree upon the rate before boarding the taxi.

The one-time capital of Selangor, Klang is completely overshadowed economically by Shah Alam. However, while Shah Alam has been planned and efficienctly built, Klang is far more colourful and exuberant. In addition, its long and proud history has left its mark on the town.

For much of its past, the Bugis, a maritime people from the Celebes Islands (now Sulawesi), played a dominant role in Klang's palace politics. In fact, Klang was one of the three capitals of the state, the other two being Kuala Langat and Kuala Selangor. As the warlords in each capital set out to establish their hegemony, conflict was inevitable. The 1867 Selangor Civil War was one of

Sultan Salahuddin Abdul Aziz Shah Mosque

the most significant developments in Klang's history. In the end, it established Klang's dominance as the state capital and, consequently, its development as a major metropolis.

Tell the taxi driver to take you around the town centre. Unlike Kuala Lumpur, Klang never went through a rash of urbanisation in which lovely old homes and shophouses were torn down and replaced with glass-and-steel cuboids. Much of Klang town still retains a lot of its old character; many buildings have been around since World War II, making it an excellent historical monuments tour.

Start your tour by telling the taxi driver to take you to **Kota Raja Mahadi** on Jalan Kota. It is a fort built by one of the protagonists in the 1867 Civil War. Across the town, along Jalan Tepi Sungai, is **Gedung Raja Abdullah**. It was built in 1856 by Raja Mahadi's opponent, Raja Abdullah, who played a key role in the founding of Kuala Lumpur through the prospecting of tin. The warehouse, which typifies traditional Malay architecture, has been converted into the Tin Museum (daily 9am–4pm), bringing back Klang's exciting past to life.

On Jalan Timur is the venerable **Sultan Sulaiman Mosque**, built by the British in the 19th century and given to Sultan Sulaiman. It has an interesting blend of British Imperial, Moorish and Arabic architectural styles. A British architect designed the mosque.

Another building that features a similar blend of architectural styles is the **Istana Alam Shah**, the palace of the Sultan of Selangor, located on Jalan Istana. The Sultan no longer resides here but in Shah Alam. However, the palace is still maintained for official functions. It is not open to the public, but is visible some 100m (330ft) to the left (as you face the main gate) from where you can enjoy a panoramic view of the palace and its grounds. Unfortunately, parking is difficult.

The above tour sequence takes you from one side of Klang town to the other. After you have finished touring the town, it should be close to late evening. Round off the day with a sumptuous seafood meal at Port Klang. Once known as Port Swettenham, it is the major seaport for Kuala Lumpur and the Klang Valley.

Tell the taxi driver to take you to the **Bagan Seafood Restaurant** (tel: 376 4546) in the Bagan Hailam area about 20 minutes by taxi from Klang. Sitting on a wooden deck by the Klang River, this well-known eatery overlooks the Royal Selangor Yacht Club and the bobbing lights of the moored boats. Its Chinese-style specialities include baked fish, chilly crab and steamed 'drunken' prawns. You even have the option of fishing for your own dinner at the commercial fish ponds outside the restaurant. Arrange for the cab to pick you up after the meal.

To get back to Kuala Lumpur, you could take the bus, a journey of about an hour which ends at the Klang Bus Station in the capital. Alternatively, take the train back. On the way, you will get a night-time view of Shah Alam and Petaling Jaya.

...ana Alam Shah

EXCURSIONS

The following excursions are designed to introduce rural Malaysia in addition to some typical attractions that visitors to Kuala Lumpur like to see. The tours range from the man-made (theme parks and a casino in Genting Highlands) to the natural (Lentang Forest) and the unusual (a community of houses built on stilts at Pulau Ketam). Most are off the well-worn tourist path and are frequented by knowing KL-ites seeking to escape their stress-filled workday week in the city.

9. Genting Highlands

Take a journey to the cool hills and enjoy the exhilaration of a highland theme park and casino.

Genting Highlands – perched on top of the Titiwangsa mountain range that runs down the centre of the peninsula – is one of Kuala Lumpur's most popular recreation destinations. It boasts a family-oriented theme park, the country's largest theatre restaurant and its only legal casino. With other attractions like an 18-hole golf

Rolling hills to Genting Highlands

A Genting Highlands resort hotel and amusement park

course, cable cars, restaurants, amusement parks and a boating lake, and given the fact that Genting Highlands is only 48km (30 miles) from Kuala Lumpur, it is little surprise that Genting Highlands gets very crowded at weekends and school holidays. Located some 2,000m (6,500ft) above sea level, the midday temperature at Genting Highlands ranges from a cool 16–23°C (60–72°F), a respite from the city heat.

There are several ways of getting to Genting Highlands. The cheapest is by air-conditioned buses from the Puduraya Bus Station. Express buses run every half hour between 7.30am–7pm (tel: 232 6863). The fare is inclusive of the 13-minute cable car ride from the base of the hill to the **Gentings Resort** at the peak. The resort comprises five hotels and apartments, all of which are inter-linked. The cable car service operates 24 hours a day.

If you're booked into the **Awana Golf and Country Resort** midway up, you take a shuttle from the base. Taxis also operate from Puduraya and deliver you directly to your hotel. Besides the golf course, Awana has splendid scenery, jungle treks and waterfalls. A shuttle links it to the resort.

Once at the resort, clear directional signs make it easy to find your way around. If you wish to enter the casino, bear in mind that patrons have to be appropriately dressed. Men are required to wear ties with long-sleeved shirts or a jacket without tie. Alternatively, the traditional Malaysian batik shirt is acceptable – these can be rented at the entrance. A sign over the entrance to the casino strictly forbids Muslims from entering, in accordance with the Islamic prohibition against gambling.

Genting's amusement park will keep non-gamblers busy. There is an indoor theme park with stunning virtual reality displays. Note: there are no cheap eateries and the only food outlets, both Western and local, are hotel restaurants and coffee shops.

10. Lentang Forest Recreation Park

Escape the city bustle and spend a day in a forest reserve.

For rainforest buffs, the **Lentang Forest Recreation Park** (Hutan Lipur Lentang), some 48km (30 miles) from Kuala Lumpur, offers many hours of relaxation. There is a clear stream that runs through the forest, complete with waterfall and a short run of rapids. Swimming is possible in some stretches. Besides picnic areas,

JABATAN HUTAN NEGERI PAHANG DARUL MAKMUR

toilets, bathing rooms and shelters, numerous hiking trails lead into the surrounding jungle.

Lentang is reached by taking the bus to Bentong from the Tun Razak Bus Station. The service is operated by the Central Pahang Omnibus Company and takes roughly an hour. Be sure to tell the conductor to warn you when to get off – the park is 16km (10 miles) before Bentong and the bus will make a stop here first. The return service to Kuala Lumpur runs every half hour. There is also a taxi service from Kuala Lumpur to Bentong.

If you are planning an extensive hike through the jungle, it might be a good idea to consult the Forest Rangers on duty at the site. The forest is home to a variety of interesting wildlife and plants. Take the opportunity to walk quietly and you may be lucky enough to see some of the animals, birds, insects and reptiles that are unique to this country. The tracks are reasonably well marked but remember to identify features so that you do not get lost. The forest rangers will be able to provide relevant information on which trails to follow and more importantly, keep a look out if you do not return on time.

Enjoy nature in Lentang Recreational Forest

Of course, the time taken for your hike will depend on how fit you are and how far you want to go, but try not to be too ambitious unless you are a seasoned hiker.

As access to food and drinks is limited in the park area, consider bringing your own from Kuala Lumpur; the other option is to patronise the Malay food stall that is located near the park entrance.

Stilt houses line Pulau Ketam's banks

11. Pulau Ketam

Relax in a fishing village and feast on some of Malaysia's most wonderful seafood.

A day trip with a difference, **Pulau Ketam** (Crab Island) is 1½ hours away by boat from **Port Klang**. When the island's intrepid pioneers discovered it about a century ago, Pulau Ketam was nothing more than a mangrove mudpile that almost disappeared during high tide. Instead of looking for greener pastures, they stayed put, building their houses on stilts. Today, a whole township, complete with sidewalks, groceries, power station, telephone exchange and bars, all on stilts, has developed on the island.

Everything on the island revolves around fishing: catching it, transporting it to the mainland, or servicing the industry. Although it is illegal for fishing vessels to carry passengers, it has not stopped the fishermen of Pulau Ketam from openly soliciting anglers.

The town's restaurants serve some of the finest seafood around. Try the **Nam Hong** or **Kim Hor** restaurants, both renowned for the island speciality, ie steamed *sembilang* or catfish. Visitors from as far away as Singapore think nothing of making their way to Pulau Ketam just for the seafood.

As Teochew and Cantonese people mainly live on the island, the cooking style is Chinese. The seafood can be cooked in various ways but it is usually not *halal* (kosher) for Muslims, so ask first.

To get to Pulau Ketam, take the train (KTM) to the Pelabuhan Klang stop and from there go to the public jetty at Port Klang. The jetty is a good place to take interesting photos of fresh fish that is constantly unloaded from the boats. Ferry services to the island start at 7am and operate every hour. The last ferry leaves the island at 6pm. There is also the option of hiring one of the fast boats; just be sure that a price has been negotiated before stepping onboard.

Ornaments made of shells

If you want to spend the night, the only billeting of any quality on Pulau Ketam is the **Ketam Island Village Lodge**. Located conveniently at the jetty, the lodge offers basic but clean and comfortable air-conditioned accommodation at very reasonable rates.

As Pulau Ketam was built to serve the needs of the local community, it is the perfect place to soak in the atmosphere of a lively fishing village. Except for a short stroll around the small

island to look at the village and a meal at the seafood restaurants, there are no other tourist attractions. Two or three hours here would be more than sufficient and will give you an insight into this busy fishing island. It is also possible to visit nearby fish farms to observe their operations, so ask around.

If you are staying overnight, there are a couple of karaoke lounges and nightclubs on the island. They are all within the immediate vicinity of the Ketam Island Village Lodge. You should be warned that the nightclub acts are known to get raunchy at times, but that has never stopped anyone from having a good time.

Away from the mayhem of city life

12. Forest Research Institute of Malaysia

Discover a tropical rainforest on the edge of the city.

The oldest jungles in the world are the tropical rainforests of Southeast Asia and South America. Looking at Kuala Lumpur today though, it is difficult to believe that the city was once covered in dense tropical rainforest. Those who wish to visit an authentic rainforest without travelling too far out of the city need not despair. Tucked away in the hills north-west of Kuala Lumpur is one of the world's oldest forest research centres. Covering some 600ha (1,480 acres), the **Forest Research Institute of Malaysia (FRIM)** is a showcase for the incredible variety of flora and fauna found within a tropical lowland forest.

Opened in 1926, FRIM has gained increasing popularity among KL-ites and visitors as a peaceful retreat from city living. Located some 16km (10 miles) from the city, it is most easily reached by taxi. There are no bus services to the institute, so arrange with your taxi driver to pick you up from FRIM later. If you're driving, you will have to pay a nominal entry charge for your car.

Once there, finding your way around the well-signposted park is easy. You may wish to pick up maps of the grounds from the public relations office. The nature trails and jungle tracks are shown on these maps, with explanations of the vegetation you can expect to see.

Since this park is dedicated to environmental science research, every attempt has been made to conserve the forest ecosystem. You would notice on your way in that all the signs, buildings and houses are environmentally-friendly and the structures appear to blend with the surroundings. Traditional wooden houses constructed without the use of nails can also be visited. There is also a museum (open daily 9am–5pm) and a nursery.

One of the most significant features of any tropical forest is its multi-canopied structure, each canopy being a sub-ecosystem in its own right. Unfortunately, this feature is among the first to disappear with tourist development. In FRIM, the authorities have taken pains to preserve the multi-tiered canopies of the forest. There is a fascinating canopy walk high above ground to allow visitors to view the upper canopy. However, the walk is only open to large groups and must be booked in advance.

After picking up literature at the public relations office, wander through the various arboretums. There are six of these, showcasing indigenous fruit trees, conifers, monocotyledenous trees, Dipterocarps and non-Dipterocarps. The trees in the various arboretums are clearly labelled so that visitors can identify what they see.

One of the must-dos at the FRIM is a walk on one of its many nature trails. The **Keruing nature trail** is the shortest, beginning behind the library and ending at the fishpond. The jungle tracks are longer and reach deeper into the forest. You will see nature in all its glory: diverse and prolific. The forest symphony comprising

Traditional wooden house built without nails

the cicada chorus accompanied by crickets and other insects will entertain you on your jaunt. The park is also a great place for bird-watching. You will see some of the more exotic Malaysian species if you move quietly through the forest.

Cool respite by the stream

There is only one cafeteria in the park, so if you're planning a hike up to the waterfall, you may want to buy food and drinks from the canteen next to the gymnasium. Alternatively, bring a packed lunch and picnic in the forest. The park organises day trips for groups of over 40 people, but such excursions have to be pre-booked. If you plan to camp overnight, obtain permission from the park authorities first.

The best time to visit the tropical forest park is in the early morning or late evening when the air is most fresh, although walking in the shady forest is usually relatively cool though humid. Remember to drink lots of water.

13. Kuala Selangor

Explore a ruined fortress, a lighthouse and a mausoleum. Go birdwatching in a nature park, enjoy a seafood meal and see the river light up with fireflies.

Standing at the estuary of the Selangor River, **Kuala Selangor** was once the capital to the Sultanate of Selangor. Back then, the river was a vital means of communication to the otherwise impenetrable interior. The Selangor River was also the key to political and economic power: those who controlled communications along the river also controlled the hinterland. The state of Selangor, in this respect, had three great river systems – the Langat, Klang and Selangor – and the respective nobilities that controlled these rivers constantly bickered for dominance. Ultimately, the group controlling the Klang became pre-eminent. Today, the Klang valley is the nation's fastest growing urban area, while both Kuala Langat and Kuala Selangor have slipped into obscurity.

What greatness the town of Kuala Selangor once knew remains in the form of ruined fortresses, lighthouses and a mausoleum. This excursion is best done in the afternoon. There are buses which travel to

Kuala Selangor Resthouse

Chalets at Kuala Selangor Nature Park

Kuala Selangor but for more flexiblity hire a taxi, especially if you want to see the fireflies in the evening. You need at least six hours, so negotiate a fair rate with the taxi driver. Alternatively, go on an organised tour. If you plan to spend the night, the **Kuala Selangor Resthouse**, an old colonial structure on Bukit Melawati, gives you a fine view of the district and the Straits of Malacca (Selat Melaka). The rates here are reasonable and simple meals are served.

Two forts were built to defend the town. The larger and the only one open to the public is **Kota Melawati** (formerly Fort Altingsburg), which stands on Bukit Melawati. It is 100m (330ft) diagonally opposite the resthouse, although vegetation obscures the view of the fort from the resthouse.

e Altingsburg Lighthouse

From the fort, you can easily walk to other interesting places nearby. Signboards along the pathways minimise the chances of getting lost. Some of the places to visit at Bukit Melawati include the **Altingsburg Lighthouse**, which is still functional, and the **Royal Mausoleum**, which enshrines the remains of Selangor's ancient Bugis kings. Either walk or drive to **Kuala Selangor Nature Park**, (tel: 03 889-2294) at the base of the hill away from the town. A nominal entry fee helps maintain the park operated by the Malaysian Nature Society. Simple chalet accommodation and facilities are available for overnight stays.

Migratory waterbirds are the main attractions here but there are monkeys and otters as well. There are stands of mangrove and secondary forest and a brackish lake system with boardwalks to provide access to the wildlife. A shop rents equipment including binoculars and sells souvenirs.

Head back to **Kuala Selangor** town, which has a few good seafood restaurants. Enjoy an early evening meal and then travel to **Kampung Kuantan**, 9km (5½ miles) south of Kuala Selangor. After 8pm, boats take visitors on a 40-minute ride on the river through trees lined with tiny luminescent fireflies. The millions of tiny male beetles flashing synchronously in the dark is an amazing sight indeed. But be sure to avoid rainy nights, as there would then be fewer fireflies to behold.

Nightlife

Kuala Lumpur's nightlife is not as racy as Manila's or Bangkok's but the action is still there for visitors who want to see a different side to the city. Known as the 'garden city of lights', Kuala Lumpur lives up to its name when the sun goes down. The city certainly has a varied nightlife, with many shops open until 10pm, and an active streetlife as well. Whether it is eating and shopping, night-clubbing or dancing at the latest hot-spots, or pub crawling, there is enough to keep you awake till the wee hours of the morning.

Night Markets

Every day, the city authorities close off a street or two to vehicles, turning the space over to small-time traders and hawkers for the evening. The *pasar malam*, or night markets, are a hallowed institution in Malaysia, bazaars filled with much exuberance and colour. The night market vendors sell everything from fresh vegetables, meat, fish, fruits and cooked food, to toys, household ware, electronics, clothes and bric-a-brac.

However, it is not just the variety of merchandise that makes the night markets special for KL-ites. The markets are social institutions as well, providing an opportunity for neighbours and friends to

A makeshift Chinese opera show at the local night market

Bargains at Chow Kit Bazaar

meet in the cool of the evening. Since night markets do not necessarily stick to the same spots, ask your hotel concierge for specific locations each evening. This information can also be obtained from the Tourist Information centres. Following are some popular night market sites in the city: **Jalan Angsana**, off Jalan Tun Sambanthan on Wednesday; **Kampung Datuk Keramat** on Friday; **Jalan Tuanku Abdul Rahman**, **Jalan Telawi Dua** and **Bangsar Baru** on Saturday; and **Taman Tun Dr Ismail** on Sunday.

Lounges

These are found in hotels and are often places where business deals are sealed over drinks or coffee. Lounges are also hot favourites with the older crowd and snuggling couples. Open in concept and furnished with comfortable sofas, the entertainment usually comprises easy listening music by a live band, more often than not Filipino, or a singer and pianist. One of the most popular and lively lounges is at the **Concorde Hotel** in Jalan Sultan Ismail; one of the most posh is **Shangri-la's**, across the road.

Dance Clubs

There are quite a few discos or dance clubs in Kuala Lumpur, ranging from the ultra-trendy where yuppies come dressed to kill, to dark seedy bars that you wouldn't want to be caught dead in. Most good hotels have dance clubs as standard fixtures. Most are open on weekdays from 5pm–1am, with happy hours ending at around 9pm; on weekends these clubs remain open till 3am or later.

The following are recommended: **TM2** at the Kuala Lumpur Hilton; **Musictheque** at the Istana; **Hard Rock Cafe** at the Concorde Hotel; **Roxy** at the Rennaisance Hotel; and **The Backroom** behind Shangri-La. The Golden Triangle club cluster at Jalan Sultan Ismail and Jalan P Ramlee area includes **The Emporium**, **Brannigan's**, **Modesto's**, and a little away in Jalan Mayang opposite the Australian High Commission, **El Nino**. In Petaling Jaya, head for hot spots like **Viva** at the Eastin Hotel in Jalan Damansara, and **Uncle Chilli's** at the PJ Hilton.

This list is by no means exhaustive. Daily newspapers and entertainment magazines like *Day and Night* carry comprehensive listings of entertainment spots around the city.

Pubs

While alcohol is not a central feature of Malaysian culture, an increasing number of office workers, businessmen and executives congregate in these watering holes after work to wash down their tribulations with a beer or two before trudging home. Most pubs serve food, the mainstay being sandwiches, chicken wings and French fries. In addition, many pubs feature live music and almost all have sound systems, playing popular tunes.

Pubs come and go all the time but the ones with staying power include the imaginatively-titled **The Pub** in Shangri-La Hotel and the beer garden, **Blues Cafe**, at Lot 10 in Bukit Bintang. **Wall Street** on Jalan P Ramlee has an intriguing concept, where drink prices rise with demand. Recently hip are cafes such as the **Benson & Hedges Bistro**, **T.G.I. Fridays**, and **Coffee Bean and Tea Leaf**, all around the Golden Triangle club cluster; and wine and cigar bars such as **Little Havana** in Cangkat Raja Chulan behind the Istana Hotel.

Head out to the trendiest suburb, Bangsar Baru, for wall-to-wall pubs. This is the place to see and be seen. **Ronnie Q's**, **The Roof**, **Soleil's**, **Big Willy's** and **Finnegan's Irish Pub** are but a few of the spots that blend outdoor chic with urban cool.

Karaoke Lounges

Kuala Lumpur's – indeed, the country's – greatest night-time passion is karaoke. Karaoke lounges here are essentially spruced up bars equipped with audio facilities that project musical lyrics and a suitable theme on a TV console while playing the instrumental background through a sophisticated hi-fi set-up. This provides the necessary environment for amateur singers to sing along in unison.

Kuala Lumpur and its suburbs are peppered with karaoke lounges, providing facilities ranging from the bare essentials, ie a microphone and sound system and little else, to luxuriously-outfitted lounges with state-of-the-art equipment.

Many restaurants also offer karaoke facilities, just as there are discos with karaoke rooms, such as **Uncle Chillie's** in the PJ Hilton, and the Hotel Istana's **Musictheque**. Some places even offer rooms decorated along themes; **Brannigan's** at Lorong Ampang has Victorian and Japanese theme rooms, while the Musictheque features rooms done up in regional Malaysian decor. Unlike in the West, most local karaoke patrons take their singing very seriously, and will not tolerate people making fun of their efforts. If you do not want to sing, avoid these bars.

Karaoke lounges may also come with 'guest relations officers' – pretty faces that offer lonely men easy conversation, join them in a drink and laugh at their jokes, however lame they may be. Overt hanky-panky is disallowed on the premises but the management generally closes an eye to whatever transactions that spring up between their guest relations officers and customers after closing.

The better karaoke lounges would include ultra high-end **Club** de Macao in Rennaisance Hotel, **Songbird** on Jalan Imbi, and **Star KTV** at the Life Centre in Jalan Sultan Ismail and Bangsar Shopping Centre, Bangsar. Opening hours are 9pm–1am weekdays, and until 2am on weekends.

Music Clubs

Although Malaysians are generally musically inclined, finding places that play good live music can be difficult. The few good spots that have bands normally feature cover versions of popular hits. Although most of the places listed below feature live acts, it is wise to call ahead and check. When no bands are in attendance, the same places have deejays playing the latest dance music.

Those into jazz should visit **Market** and its branch at Phileo Damansara, Petaling Jaya (near Eastin Hotel). **Blues Cafe** on Lot 10 Jalan Bukit Bintang also features live jazz.

Hard Rock Cafe, in the Concorde Hotel, **The Emporium** down the road, and **Uncle Chilie's** in PJ Hilton sometimes feature live groups. Damansara Utama, in Petaling Jaya, has over 30 pubs, some featuring good bands. **Blue Moon** in Equatorial Hotel plays oldies but goodies from the 1950s, while Kuala Lumpur Hilton's **TM2** band belts out favourites from the 1960s to the 1980s.

For canto-pop (Chinese language hits), head for **Halo Cafe** at Jalan Balai Polis in Chinatown. The more hard core riffs can grab a drink at **Halo Rock Cafe** at the end of the block.

Theatre

There is a small but active theatre scene in Kuala Lumpur, with plays held infrequently at the **Dewan Bandaraya** on Jalan Raja Laut, **Panggung Eksperimen** off Jalan Parlimen, **The Actor's Studio** beneath Dataran Merdeka, and the **Malaysian Tourist Information Centre (MATIC)** on Jalan Ampang. For details, check the dailies or with the Actor's Studio (tel: 294 5400).

Cultural shows are also held occasionally at MATIC and **Central Market**, usually for free. The top classical concert venue is the **Dewan Filharmonik Petronas** theatre in the KLCC (tel: 207 7007).

Central Market

Eating Out

Kuala Lumpur is probably not the best place in the world to start dieting. The variety of food is endless, the portions large and the prices reasonable. In the end, it is probably wiser to let your epicurean urges go wild and sample what the city has to offer. Leave your dieting for when you get home. You have a choice of Malay, Chinese, Indian, Nonya food, besides French, Mexican, Spanish, Italian, Japanese and Korean cuisines. Even the major cuisines have sub-types that are radically different. With 13 states and culinary specialities within each region, the array of Malay food is almost infinite. As for Chinese food, every provincial variety is available, be it Cantonese, Hokkien, Teochew or Hainanese.

Some of the dishes have become so localised they can only be labelled Malaysian, such as *bak-kut-teh*, pork stewed in a soup of five-spice powder and coriander. The so-called Nonya food is a delicious hybrid of Chinese and Malay cuisines. Indian food covers the spectrum of South Indian, Punjabi, Moghul and Indian-Muslim dishes. There are also different ways of cooking the same foods: seafood, a Malaysian favourite, can be done Chinese or Malay style, while vegetarian food has both Chinese and Indian varieties.

If the range of cuisines hasn't excited your tastebuds, then perhaps the varied locations in which the food is served might. These range from fine continental restaurants to the street stalls

All you ever need to quench your thirst

which come alive every evening on most street corners. The quality of the food, however, has nothing to do with where it is served. Some of Kuala Lumpur's best food comes from hawkers whose clientele includes people from all walks of life. Don't fret if some of the stalls do not appear to be clean: many Malaysians routinely eat from these stalls without ever falling sick.

Chillies are the heart of fiery Malaysian curries

Hawker food is something no visitor should miss while in Kuala Lumpur. Not only do hawkers serve a variety of authentic local dishes, prices are also very reasonable and hawker-stall dining is an experience on its own. Although roadside stalls are a common sight, the modernisation of the city has swept many of these hawkers into the concrete, air-conditioned food arcades in shopping malls (see listing under *Hawker Centres* for their locations).

Open-air hawker centres are scattered all over the city and some of the larger ones are in Petaling Street (mostly Chinese food); Jalan Bunus (mainly Malay and Indonesian food); Jalan Alor (Chinese/Penang food); Brickfields (mixed local food but mainly Indian); Chow Kit (mostly Malay food); Jalan Kampung Attap, along Jalan Imbi (Chinese Malaysian); Subang Jaya (mixed); Jalan SS2 in Petaling Jaya (mixed); and Damansara Uptown, Damansara Utama, PJ (Malay and Chinese).

Food vendors also group together in shop lots on every other street. Some hawkers keep going till 2 or 3am and there are others who even keep their stalls open till dawn. Bangsar Baru stalls are particularly popular among the young crowd returning from a night of partying.

The restaurant list on the following pages is by no means exhaustive; entire books have been devoted to the topic. Price categories for a meal for two without drinks are categorised as:

$ = under RM30; $$ = RM30–80; $$$ = RM80 and above.

Malay

NASI LEMAK BENTENG UTAMA
Jalan Bunus 1 (Masjid India area)
A dinner-only riverside stall that sells fragrant coconut milk rice with spicy dishes; try the potato cutlets, curry chicken and beef *rendang*. $

NELAYAN RESTAURANT
Taman Tasik Titiwangsa
Tel: 422 8400
Offering typical Malay cuisine, specialising in "steamboat". $

PAYA SERAI RESTAURANT
PJ Hilton
Tel: 755 9122
Buffet selection of Malay, Chinese and Indian dishes. Good for those wary of hawker food. $$

RASA UTARA
Bukit Bintang Plaza
Jalan Bukit Bintang
Tel: 248 8639
Specialises in northern Malay cuisine. Try the *ayam percik*, a hot, sour chicken dish which has made the state of Kelantan proud. $$

SERI MELAYU
1 Jalan Conlay
Tel: 245 1833
Located in a large wooden traditional house, the restaurant serves good Malay food accompanied by a cultural performance. $$

Chinese

COSY CORNER
1st Floor, Ampang Park
Tel: 261 5649
Wide variety of tasty Malaysian and Cantonese dishes. $

ESQUIRE KITCHEN
Level 1 Sungai Wang Plaza
Jalan Sultan Ismail
Tel: 261 7777
Budget dumplings and pork dishes are main draw of this centrally-located restaurant. $

GOLDEN PHOENIX RESTAURANT
Hotel Equatorial, Jalan Sultan Ismail
Tel: 261 7777
Serves mainly Cantonese cuisine using only the freshest of ingredients. Dishes to try include the sizzling venison, sharks fin soup, braised abalone and salt-baked prawns. $$$

HAI TIEN LO
Pan Pacific Hotel

Preserved duck eggs

Chinese sponge cakes

Tel: 442 5555
Cantonese and Szechuan Chinese cuisine, all *halal* (kosher). $$$

HAKKA RESTAURANT
off Jalan Maarof
Bangsar Baru
Tel: 282 4211
Specialises in Hakka food, which features lots of braised meat dishes. $$

MARCO POLO RESTAURANT
1st Floor, Wisma Lim Foo Yong
Jalan Raja Chulan
Tel: 241 2233
Traditional Cantonese cuisine. Try their specialities: the steamed fish and prawn cake wrapped in bamboo shoot. $$

MING PALACE
Ming Court Vista Hotel
Jalan Ampang
Tel: 232 2388
Try the Peking duck carved right at your table. $$

MUSEUM CHINE RESTAURANT
Legend Hotel
The Mall Putra Place
Tel: 442 9888
Fine dining in lovely ambience, with Teochew specialties including prawns and chicken. $$$

NEW FORMOSA RESTAURANT
46 Jalan SS 2/24,
Petaling Jaya

Tel: 775 7478
Serves Taiwanese food, known especially for steamboat – a do-it-yourself meal of raw meats and greens cooked in a boiling cauldron of rich stock. $$

OVERSEA RESTAURANT
Central Market
Tel: 274 6407
Good Cantonese cuisine; try the pork ribs and chilly *kung pao* chicken. $$

RESTORAN SZECHUAN
42–3 Jalan Sultan Ismail
Tel: 248 2806
Szechuan cooking is spicy, with lots of chillies and pepper. The squid fried in cashew nuts and chilli-fried shrimps are especially recommended. $$

SHANG PALACE
Shangri-La Hotel
Jalan Sultan Ismail
Tel: 232 2388
One of the best Chinese restaurants in the city with good *dim sum* for lunch. Recommended are the steamed pork buns. $$$

South Indian

DEVI'S CORNER RESTAURANT
Jalan Telawi 1, Bangsar Baru
Traditional South Indian breads and rice-and-curry dishes on a banana leaf. $

KRISHNA CURRY HOUSE
10 Jalan SS 51A/222, PJ
Tel: 756 4920
Highly rated among knowing gourmets. Known for its mutton and vegetable dishes. $

North Indian/ Pakistani

BANGLES
60A Jalan Tuanku Abdul Rahman
Tel: 298 3780
One of the city's oldest North Indian restaurants, with kitschy decor – including bangles and mirrors. Tasty food; try the *kurmas*. $$

BILAL RESTAURANT
33 Jalan Ampang
Tel: 238 0804
Another very old restaurant. This began as an offshoot of the Federal Bakeries, at one time the city's largest producer of bread. $

Healthy vegetarian food

BOMBAY PALACE
388 Jalan Tun Razak
Tel: 245 4241
In a smart bungalow with nice ambience and gracious staff. Try royal banquet of tandoori or vegetarian dishes. $$$

GEM RESTAURANT
Jalan Tun Sambanthan
Brickfields
Sample their *naan* bread with *masala* or tandoori chicken, along with their tea. $$

TAJ RESTAURANT
Crown Princess Hotel
Tel: 262 5522
Upmarket establishment and one of the more exclusive North Indian restaurants in Kuala Lumpur. Live Indian music while you dine. $$$

Vegetarian

ANNALAKSHMI RESTAURANT
44–46 Jalan Maarof
Bangsar Baru
Tel: 282 3799
The city's most famous Indian vegetarian restaurant. $$

A South Indian banana leaf meal

GOVINDA'S
16-1 Lorong Bunus Enam
Tel: 298 6785
Vedic cuisine (no meat, fish, eggs or milk) in little India. Try the pumpkin masala, taufu sambal and pakora (vegetables fried in batter). $

WAN FO YUAN
8 Jalan Panggung, Chinatown
Tel: 238 0952
Good bean curd dishes, centrally located to Petaling Street. $

Nonya

BON TON RESTAURANT
7 Jalan Kia Peng
Tel: 241 3614
A restaurant in a converted bungalow under rain trees. Creative Western and local dishes. $$

DONDANG SAYANG
Lower Ground Floor, The Weld
Tel: 261 3831
Good for the Enche Kebin chicken, and *otak-otak* baked fish. $$

KAPITAN'S CLUB
35 Jalan Ampang
Tel: 201 0242
Good nonya dishes. Try top hats, ayam Kapitan and Portugese baked fish. $$

Thai

ROM MAI
16 Jalan Pinang
Tel: 242 3080
Thai house delights include spicy prawns with herbs, and deep fried minced meat in beancurd. $$

THAI CORNER
12 Jalan Telawi 4, Bangsar Baru
Tel: 284 1607
Good selection. Try the tasty green chicken curry and chicken in pandan leaf. $

Seafood

BANGSAR SEAFOOD VILLAGE
3 Jalan Telawi Empat
Lot 4387
Tel: 282 2555
Open-air restaurant serving seafood cooked Chinese style. $$

EDEN VILLAGE
Jalan Raja Chulan
Tel 241 4027, and
EDEN GARDENIA
Jalan SS22/23, Petaling Jaya
Tel: 719 3184
Both belong to a chain of seafood restaurants. Local seafood as well as imported lobsters, oysters and salmon. Most of the food is cooked continental style. $$

HAPPY VALLEY SEAFOOD VILLAGE
18 Jalan Delima,
off Jalan Imbi
Tel: 242 2625
Sample the extensive selection of Cantonese seafood dishes offered here. $$

KAMPUNG KU SEAFOOD
Damansara Town Centre
Damansara Heights
Tel: 254 5313
Offers food dished out in various cooking styles. Famous for its baked bamboo fish. $$

KAM YING SEAFOOD
14 Jalan Telawi 4
Bangsar Baru
Good food at reasonable rates has made this restaurant Bangsar's most popular Chinese eatery. $

KELANA SEAFOOD CENTRE
Jalan Perbandaran
Kelana Jaya
A myriad of fresh seafood dishes for both lunch and dinner are found here. $$

Japanese

CHIKUYO-TEI
Basement, Plaza See Hoy Chan
Tel: 230 0729
One of the city's first Japanese restaurants. Quality food and fast service. $$$

EDO KIRIN
Regent Hotel, Jalan Bukit Bintang
Tel: 241 8000
Reputed for its fresh food and *shasshimi.* $$$

ENAGIKU
2nd Floor, Podium Block
203 Jalan Bukit Bintang
Tel: 248 2133
Cosy restaurant with Japanese-style seating. $$

GENJI
PJ Hilton, 2 Jalan Barat
Tel: 755 9122
The house specialities are California rolls and *shabu shabu.* $$

KAMPACHI
Equatorial Hotel
Jalan Sultan Ismail
Tel: 261 7777
Known for the quality and freshness of its food. Book ahead for the popular Sunday buffet. $$$

Western

CIAO
428, Jalan Tun Razak
(near RHB Bank)
Tel: 985 4827
Excellent Italian pasta and pizza in a lovely bungalow setting. $$$

CITRUS
Jalan Sultan Ismail
(opposite Concorde Hotel)
Tel: 242 5188
Specialising in so-called cross-cultural East-West cuisine. $$

COLISEUM CAFE
98 Jalan Tuanku Abdul Rahman
Tel: 292 6270
A historical landmark. Sunday tiffin of chicken curry is especially recommended. $$

DOME
Jalan Bukit Bintang
Tel: 243 4140
The best coffee in town. Light meals of *focaccias*, pasta and salads. $$

FLAMENCO
1st Floor, KL Plaza
Tel: 245 2213
Bright decor, Mediterranean food including *tapas* and *paella.* $$$

HARD ROCK CAFE
Wisma Concorde
Jalan Sultan Ismail
Tel: 244 2200
Tested formula: rock memorabilia, American food and loud music. $$

JAKE'S CHARBROIL STEAKS
21 Jalan Setiapuspa
Medan Damansara
Tel: 254 5677
Serves good Mexican starters and is well-known for its grilled fish and steaks. $$

LE COQ D'OR
Jalan Ampang
Tel: 261 9732
Chops and fish and chips in a beautiful colonial bungalow. $$

LES TABLEAUX
38 Jalan Walter Grenier
Tel: 245 9504
Excellent French-Belgian cuisine, you can bring your own wine. $$$

MAHSURI
Carcosa Sri Negara
Jalan Taman Tasik Perdana

Bright lights will beckon diners

Tel: 282 1888
Excellent high tea spread and elegant Italian dining. $$$

MODESTO'S
12A Jalan Telawi 3
Bangsar Baru
Tel: 284 2445, 284 2446
Also in Jalan P Ramlee. A good spread of antipasto, pastas, pizzas and not-to-be-missed tiramisu. $$

TGI FRIDAY'S
Ground floor Life Centre
Jalan Sultan Ismail
Tel: 263 7761
Tex-Mex cuisine. $$

THE MANGO TREE
4 Lorong Maarof, Bangsar Utama
Tel: 284 6268
This Western/Italian restaurant has an imaginative menu and beautifully presented food. $$$

THE SHIP
Jalan Sultan Ismail
Tel: 241 8805
Tasty steaks, chops, and fish and chips in a nautical setting. Branches throughout the city. $$

Hawker Centres

CENTRAL MARKET
All types of local and fast food. Especially good are the fried *char kway teow* (flat rice noodles tossed in a spicy sweet black sauce) and *Hokkien mee*, yellow wheat noodles in a rich pork-based stock.

FOOD COURT
Top floor, Kota Raya
Shopping Complex
A good mix of local fare.

HAWKER'S CENTRE
Top Floor, Sungai Wang Plaza
Mainly Malay and Chinese food.

JALAN ALUR
Bukit Bintang
Authentic Penang fare at dinnertime all in one street.

JALAN RAJA ALANG
Kampung Bahru
Mainly Malay food.

MEDAN HANG TUAH
4th floor of The Mall
Local food sold in surroundings reminiscent of KL in the 1930s.

Shopping

Kuala Lumpur is fast catching up with Singapore, Hong Kong and Bangkok as a shopper's paradise. It also offers some marvellous opportunities for craft collectors and bargain hunters. Worthwhile finds range from antiques and imported spices to religious icons and metalware. Although the law requires retail outlets to affix price tags for all goods sold, bargaining is still an integral part of the Malaysian shopping experience, so be prepared to haggle except in department stores.

Traditional Fabrics

One would have thought that gold fabric was a creation of Grecian fables. In Malaysia, it is grounded in reality, and called *songket*. Handed down from the courts of Kelantan and Pattani, this cloth is a display of dramatic handwoven tradition featuring intricate tapestry inlaid with gold and metallic threads.

Women in some parts of the Peninsula's East Coast still use the traditional two-paddle floor looms to painstakingly interlace threads, with the best pieces coming from Kelantan. *Songket* comes in a multitude of colours that offset the rich tapestry designs, its richness making it more suitable for formal and ceremonial attire. *Songket* material can also be turned into stunning jackets, beautiful evening wear and attractive handbags and shoes.

Browse around for an antique

Songket – tapestries inlaid with gold threads

Batik, the less glamourous cousin of *songket*, has more appeal because of its versatility, durability and price. In fact, *batik* techniques have become so popular, they have become an art form. Also originally from the East Coast, *batik* is now printed by factories all over the country, which produces fabrics ranging from cotton and voile to silk and satin. *Batik* is often turned into clothes, accessories, household and decorative items.

Silvercraft and Pewterware

Kelantan silvercraft is one of the most successful cottage industries in Malaysia. It is a craft requiring sharp skills, whether in filigree work, where ornamental wire is shaped into delicate tracery, or repousses, where sheet silver is hammered into patterned relief. Kelantan silver is turned into a variety of items, from brooches and costume jewellery to serving dishes and tableware.

Kuala Lumpur's own local handicraft, Royal Selangor pewterware, enjoys a worldwide reputation for its stylish and attractive handmade designs. Pewter is an alloy of tin mixed with a little copper and antimony and was introduced to Malaysia in the last century. The hardness of the metal gives it durability, and its silvery finish does not tarnish. Using traditional methods of casting and soldering, hundreds of items ranging from tableware, candelabra and ornamental pieces to lapel pins, figurines and pendants are crafted.

Kites and Tops

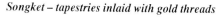

The traditional *wau* and *gasing* (kites and tops), for which the Peninsula's East Coast is best known, enjoy both local and international popularity. Both are traditional sports, with kite flying dating back to the 1500s.

The *wau* comes in all shapes and sizes. The most popular and the largest is the *wau bulan* or moon kite, measuring 3½m (11½ft) from head to tail and capable of soaring to great heights. Its wooden frame is covered with stiff parchment decorated with designs cut from coloured paper and adorned with colourful streamers. Smaller versions are made as decorative items. Malaysia Airlines, the national airline, uses one in its logo.

Top spinning is no child's play either, not when the traditional Malay top is about the size of a dinner plate and weighs as much as 5½kg (12lbs). The tops are usually disc shaped, and are carefully balanced for spinning power. A good top in the hands of a skillfull player can spin for up to two hours.

Cane, Bamboo and Straw Products, and Beadwork

Cane and wicker are used for furniture and household items. *Mengkuang* (pandanus) leaves are woven into mats, baskets, hats and decorative items, and split bamboo strips are shaped into trays, baskets and food covers.

In Sarawak, nipah palm reeds are woven into decorative mats, and rattan is used to make mats and baskets of exceptional durability. A good mat is said to last up to 30 years.

Beadwork, traditional to the native people of Sabah and Sarawak, is extremely attractive when sewn onto headbands, necklaces, belts, buttons and baskets.

Pandanus (mengkuang) leaf products

Gold

Gold has an allure that transcends international boundaries and Malaysia is no exception. Actually, where gold jewellery is concerned, there are four major traditions at work here, ie Malay, Western, Chinese and Indian.

Malay, Chinese and Indian goldsmiths tend to use pure gold (up to 24 karat) in fabricating jewellery, as opposed to Western jewellers, who combine gold with other precious metals. Even the designs are different. Malay and Indian jewellery has a distinctly religious feel. Dragon motifs and the use of jade are common features in Chinese jewellery.

The major gold retailers in the city are: Poh Kong Jewellers in The Mall, Lee Cheong Jewellers at Jalan Tun H S Lee, Abdul Razak Goldsmith at Lebuh Ampang, and international jewellers such as Selberan with outlets in Lot 10, The Mall and Yow Chuan Plaza, and P H Henry at Jalan Tuanku Abdul Rahman.

Clothing

Good quality cottons, linens and silks, either made locally or im-

There is no business like shoe business

Ethnic goods for sale at Central Market

ported, are fashioned into ready-to-wear clothing. For the finicky, made-to-measure clothes by trained tailors are also available. Boutiques offer exclusive designs that can be customised for your requirements. Prices here, however, are generally higher.

Miscellaneous

Cameras, pens, watches and mini stereo systems are relatively inexpensive as they are exempted from import duty. A wide variety is available, and retail outlets can be found in all the large shopping complexes. On the other hand, imported goods such as cosmetics and electronic items can be expensive. Locally made leather goods, however, are a worthwhile buy. In fact, many leading fashion houses like Charles Jourdan and Gucci have their products made by Malaysian manufacturers.

Where to Buy

The best Malaysian handicrafts, unfortunately, are not found in Kuala Lumpur, but in their home states. A good variety, however, can be found in the **Kompleks Budaya Kraf** on Jalan Conlay and in the shops at **Central Market**. Pewterware can be purchased in major department stores and the **Royal Selangor Pewter** showroom in Cheras, where there are factory tours too.

The popular Lot 10

Bukit Bintang shophouses add to the local colour

There are many shops that sell *batik* and *songket* in Jalan Tun Perak, and it is a good idea to check these out at the **Jalan Tuanku Abdul Rahman** and **Masjid India** areas, as well as the bazaars in **Kampung Bahru** and **Jalan Raja Laut.**

Shops in **Masjid India, Jalan Melayu** and **Lorong Bugus** also sell textiles, clothes, religious paraphernalia, metalware and handicrafts from countries such as India, Pakistan, the Middle East and Indonesia. Browse through these specialty shops and you will find value-for-money items.

Chinatown, naturally, is the place for Chinese and Taiwanese goods such as herbs, spices and Taoist prayer items. Equally ubiquitous in Chinatown are shops and sidewalk vendors that stock cheap clothing – albeit with fake brand names – shoes, toys, crockery and other household items. These stalls are also interspersed with sidewalk vendors from exotic destinations like Nepal and Russia, who sell a range of unusual merchandise.

For better quality and designer labels, the best bet would be the large shopping complexes. Good places to shop include **Lot 10, Sungei Wang Plaza, Bukit Bintang Plaza, Star Hill** and **KL Plaza** in Bukit Bintang; **Imbi Plaza** in the same area for computer and electronics buffs; **Suria KLCC, Ampang Park, Yow Chuan Plaza** and **City Square** along Jalan Ampang; **Sogo** and **Globe Silk Store** on Jalan Tuanku Abdul Rahman and **Pertama Complex** on the same road for leather and budget goods; **The Mall** on Jalan Putra; and **The Weld** on Jalan Raja Chulan. Outside of the town centre, try the **Bangsar Shopping Complex** in Bangsar, **1 Utama** in Bandar Utama and **Jaya's (Section 14)** and **Subang Parade** in Petaling Jaya.

Snacks galore

Calendar of Special Events

The multi-ethnic mix in Malaysia – a blend of Malays, Chinese, Indians, Eurasians and at least 30 other indigenous and other ethnic groups – weaves a social fabric embroidered with tradition, variety and colour. Auspicious occasions and festivals of religious and cultural significance of each group take place throughout the year, in consonance with different calendar systems.

Malaysians observe an 'open house' tradition during these festivities, inviting friends and relatives to their homes to indulge in that great Malaysian pastime – eating.

A good many festival dates are not fixed as they shift annually, depending on the lunar and Muslim calendars. Check with Tourist Information Centres for the exact dates of celebrations.

JANUARY/FEBRUARY

Thaipusam (January/February): Commemorates the handing over of the *vale* (trident) of virtue to the Hindu deity, Lord Subramaniam. It is celebrated by Hindus all over the country with great fervour. Thousands converge at one of the holiest Hindu shrines at Batu Caves to offer thanks and pray, many of them bearing *kavadi*, a wooden framed structure designed to carry containers of milk and rose water, as offerings. Sometimes the procession takes on a macabre dimension, with skewers pierced into the body of the *kavadi* bearers. The crowds start gathering the evening before when the statue of Lord Subramaniam is drawn by chariot from the Sri Mahamariamman Temple on Jalan Bandar to the temple cave. *Kavadi*-bearers generally begin their 272-step climb at dawn, but devotees throng the temple the whole day.

Deities adorn Sri Mahamariamman Temple

Federal Territory Day (February 1): Kuala Lumpur brings out the fireworks, streamers and balloons to celebrate its birthday. Special events, from cultural and musical performances to water sports, take place throughout the day.

Chinese New Year (January/February): This important Chinese festival heralds the first moon of the lunar new year, and is marked by prayers, reunion dinners and lion dances. Although only two days are designated as public holidays, most Chinese-owned shops close for up to five days. Chinatown is at its best before the celebration. Join the crowds in their last-minute shopping on the eve at Jalan Petaling and try the festive goodies, many of which are imported from China.

Wesak Day (May/June): The most significant festival for Buddhists commemorates the birth, enlightenment and death of Lord Buddha. Temples are packed with devotees offering prayers and giving alms to the monks. Visit the International Buddhist Pagoda along Jalan Berhala, Brickfields, or the temple off Jalan Gasing in Petaling Jaya. The air is usually filled with the smell and smoke from giant joss-sticks on the temple grounds, compounded by that from the hundreds of joss-sticks raised in prayer by constant streams of devotees to the statue of Lord Buddha and other deities. Worshippers receive yellow strings from the monks to be worn around their wrists for luck.

AUGUST

Merdeka Day (August 31): Malaysia's Hari Kebangsaan (National Day) is celebrated with a mammoth parade at Dataran Merdeka along Jalan Raja. Here, in 1957, the declaration of independence was made. The parade starts at 7 or 8am, and is difficult to view unless you go to the square very early. Alternatively, watch it on TV. Roads in the immediate vicinity are closed to traffic.

SEPTEMBER

Malaysia Fest (September): A lavish two-week fete of regional festivities, foods and handicrafts held in hotels and large shopping complexes in Kuala Lumpur.

OCTOBER/NOVEMBER

Deepavali (October/November): Also known as the Festival of Lights, this falls in the Tamil month of Aipassi. Hindus celebrate the triumph of good over evil with prayers, and line their gardens with oil lamps to receive blessings from Lakshmi,

National Day parade

the Goddess of Wealth. Another 'open house' affair.

DECEMBER

Christmas (December 25) is celebrated with imitation fir trees, carolling in shopping malls, and midnight masses in churches. Shopping complexes and hotels take the lead with their decorations, complete with sleighs and 'snow'.
Variable: **Hari Raya Puasa**, which celebrates the first day of the Muslim month of Shawal, follows a month of strict fasting and prayers known as Ramadan. The start of the fasting period is governed by the Muslim calendar. Muslims usher in Hari Raya Puasa by attending prayers, followed with 'open house' the whole day long, for guests to feast on delicious home-cooked Malay food, cakes and cookies.

Right, National Day light-up

Practical Information

MALAYSIA

GETTING THERE

By Rail

The main train line from Singapore to Bangkok and beyond passes through the Stesen Keretapi Kuala Lumpur (Kuala Lumpur Railway Station). The KTM Berhad trains are modern and the service is efficient. Travellers generally take the express services, which are faster because they make a minimal number of stops. There are three classes of service. Most trains are air-conditioned and have buffet cars serving simple meals. Videos keep most passengers entertained but can be disturbing to those who want to sleep, read or simply enjoy the scenery. Sleeping berths are available on long distance trains. These are a comfortable and cheap source of accommodation for those on a budget. There are day and night trains to both Singapore and Butterworth in Penang. From Butterworth, there are train connections to the north into Thailand.

For more information, call 273 8000.

Several times weekly, the luxurious **Eastern and Oriental Express** makes a brief, late night stop at the Railway Station. Completely refurbished to the tune of US$30 million, the train is an attempt to re-create rail travel of a bygone era. The cream-and-green coloured trains carry up to 130 passengers from Singapore to Kuala Lumpur and Butterworth, terminating in Bangkok (and vice versa). Passengers may embark at any of these points. Whatever route you decide on, rest assured it will burn a huge hole in your pockets. For reservations call: Malaysia Tel: 03-781 1337, Singapore Tel: 65-323 4390, Thailand Tel: 662-216 5939.

By Sea

Kuala Lumpur's closest seaport is Pelabuhan Klang (Port Klang), about 40km (25 miles) away, and linked to it by highways, buses and the KTM Komuter electric train service. Ferries from Sumatra, Indonesia, dock here; smaller ferries travel daily here from Tanjong Balai near Medan. Port Klang is the main port of call for regional cruise ships, and less regularly, the international liners.

By Road

The North-South highway from Singapore to the Thai border provides a convenient means of travel through Peninsular Malaysia, the entire trip taking about 12 hours by car one way. Try and avoid crossing the border on Friday afternoons and during public holidays because of the traffic congestion at the checkpoints.

Long distance buses and taxis also travel to and from Kuala Lumpur to most destinations on the peninsula as well as Singapore and Thailand. The interstate bus stations are at Puduraya near Chinatown, and Putra and Pekeliling near the Mall. Long distance air-conditioned express buses are fast, economical and comfortable, with video entertainment on board. The buses make occasional stops for drinks, meals and toilet breaks.

Long distance taxis also leave from Puduraya. Share the cost with three other passengers or if you are in a hurry or don't want to travel with strangers, pay for the whole taxi. Most 'teksi' are diesel-powered Mercedes and have air-conditioning.

By Air

The Kuala Lumpur International Airport (KLIA) is located 70km (43 miles) south of the city in Sepang and is one of Asia's biggest and most modern airports. Planes arrive and depart from four satellite arms, which are linked to the main terminal building via an aerotrain. Domestic flights operate from the Sultan Abdul Aziz Shah Airport in Subang, barring selected sectors with international connections.

KLIA houses the national carrier **Malaysia Airlines (MAS)**, Tel: 746 3000 (24 hours), which provides both international and domestic connections to destinations on the peninsula and East Malaysia. MAS flies to and from every continent except Antarctica.

Other domestic carriers include **Pelangi Air**, **Berjaya Air** and **Air Asia**. Internal airfares are set by the government but cheaper international fares can be negotiated with travel agents. Kuala Lumpur is reputed to be a good place to buy cheap international fares. In addition to MAS, Kuala Lumpur is also well-connected by international carriers.

MAS has discounted fares on some domestic flights but this means travelling at inconvenient times. If interested you should ask for their 'night tourist fares'. Discounted student and group fares (minimum three) are also available. Note: All domestic and international

flights on MAS, except those to Japan, are non-smoking.

Departure tax on international flights is RM40 while that of domestic flights is RM10. Tickets purchased in Malaysia will include the tax, while those purchased outside the country, probably will not. If so, you will be asked for the money at the check-in counter.

Arriving in Kuala Lumpur on an international flight is easy, with all signs in both Bahasa Malaysia and English. You have to declare how much money you bring into and out of the country. Note that possession of drugs is a capital offence.

For the airport limousine service, buy a coupon with fixed fares for your destination but this is expensive if you're alone (toll-free Tel: 1-800-880-737). Buses depart from the basement every 15 minutes to Hentian Duta, 1 hour away; from where you can catch a bus or taxi to town. Buses also go to the Subang Jaya (every 1 hour) and Nilai KTM commuter train stations (every 30 minutes) where you can catch a train into town. Accommodation and car hire facilities are also available at the airport. City taxis cannot legally pick up passengers at the airport, but you can catch any cab from the city to the airport — the fare is based on mileage plus a surcharge.

TRAVEL ESSENTIALS

When to Visit

Kuala Lumpur is hot and humid. Daytime temperatures can reach a high of

A multicultural population

33°C (91°F) while the nights can be balmy, with the temperature dropping by as much as 10°C (18°F), although most times, the difference is slight. Humidity is almost always above 80 percent. As the city has no defined seasonal weather patterns, a visit can be planned for any time of the year. The central mountain range keeps out the worst of the north-east monsoon (November–February), and the city's inland location protects it from the south-west monsoon (July–September).

Kuala Lumpur gets its share of heavy rain though, with downpours and flash floods, mostly in the afternoon and early evening.

Visas

Requirements change, so check with the relevant Malaysian embassy/consulate before travelling. At time of press, citizens of the Commonwealth and ASEAN, Ireland, Switzerland, the Netherlands, San Marino and Liechtenstein do not need a visa to visit.

The following nationals do not need a visa for a visit not exceeding three months: Austria, Australia, Belgium, Italy, Japan, South Korea, Tunisia, the United States, Germany, France, Norway, Sweden, Denmark, Belgium, Finland, Luxembourg and Iceland. Citizens of Bulgaria, Rumania, Russia (C.I.S.) and Yugoslavia are allowed a seven-day visa-free visit.

Immigration requests that travellers have passports that are valid for at least six months at time of entry.

Tourist visas may be extended by applying at the **Immigration Department**, Block 1, Pusat Bandar Damansara, Damansara Heights (8am–4.15pm Monday–Friday, 8am –12.45pm Saturday).

Vaccinations

A yellow fever vaccination is required if arriving from an infected country.

Clothing

Clothes should be light and loose so pack cottons and natural fibres, instead of synthetics. Sunglasses, sun block and umbrellas are advisable. Shoes should be removed before entering temples and homes, so slip-ons are handy.

Electricity

Power supply is 220 or 240 volts at 50 Hz cycle. Most outlets use the three-pin, flat-pronged plugs and many hotels have 110-volt shaving sockets.

Time Differences

Kuala Lumpur is 8 hours ahead of GMT and 16 hours ahead of US Pacific Standard Time.

GETTING ACQUAINTED

Geography and Population

Malaysia's land mass of 330,434sq km (127,000sq miles) covers the Malay Peninsula and a third of Borneo. It is one of the world's largest producers of rubber and palm oil, in addition to producing substantial amounts of petroleum, pepper and tropical hardwoods. On the manufacturing side, the country is also the world's largest exporter of semi-conductors, rubber gloves and condoms, and the second largest exporter of air-conditioners.

Kuala Lumpur, the nation's capital, is situated about halfway down the west coast of the peninsula and 35km (22 miles) inland. Dubbed Malaysia's Garden City of Lights, it started as a riverine trading post at the confluence of the Klang and Gombak rivers over a century ago. Kuala Lumpur has since grown to a metropolis with an area of

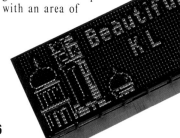

about 234sq km (89sq miles) populated by over two million inhabitants.

Malaysia's 21-million population comprises mostly Malays, Dayaks, Muruts, Bidayuhs, Kadazans, Orang Asli and about 30 other cultures of Melano-Polynesian stock, followed by substantial numbers of Chinese and Indians as well as smaller numbers of Portuguese, Eurasians and others. The Chinese largely belong to the Cantonese, Hokkien and Hakka dialect groups. The Indians consist mainly of Tamils, followed by significant numbers of Malayalis, Punjabis and Sindhis.

Government and Economy

As an ex-British colony, the legal and economic systems trace their origins to England. Although the sultan of each state still plays a role within the country, this role is becoming increasingly ceremonial. The political system is a constitutional monarchy with the King, or the Yang di-Pertuan Agong, elected every five years on a rotational basis by the 11 peninsular state rulers. The current Yang Di-Pertuan Agong is also the Sultan of Selangor.

Malaysia comprises 13 states located on the peninsula along with Sarawak and Sabah in East Malaysia on the island of Borneo. In addition, there is the Federal Territory comprising Kuala Lumpur and the international offshore financial centre of Labuan.

There are two houses of parliament; the lower house or Dewan Rakyat, and the senate or Dewan Negara. Some of the latter are appointed by the Yang di-Pertuan Agong while others are elected by the legislatures of individual states. Members are elected every five years and the current government is a coalition of Barisan National parties with the Prime Minister being Dato' Seri Dr Mahathir Mohamad. State governments are elected for the same period of office but there is no upper house.

Before the Asian economic meltdown in 1997, Malaysia's GNP growth averaged 8 percent for a decade. The Tiger Nation was well on its way to achieving its goal of developed nation status by 2020. The major shift from agriculture to manufacturing pushed the country into the top 20 largest trading nations in the world. The devaluation of the ringgit and the loss of two-thirds of its market capitalisation has taken out some of its biting ambition, with the country now struggling to achieve 1–2 percent GDP growth.

Still, unemployment remains low al-

though inflation is climbing, and economic resuscitation includes stabilising the ringgit and stimulating domestic demand and external demand for Malaysia's exports. A key investment-attracting tool is the ambitious information technology-based Multimedia Super Corridor (MSC) project. Malaysia's main exports are electrical and electronic goods, manufactured goods, textiles, clothing and footwear, palm oil, natural gas and petroleum.

How Not to Offend

Shoes should be removed before entering a Malaysian home or place of worship. When in a mosque, visitors who are inappropriately dressed should put on a robe, which will be provided, and cover their limbs. Women should avoid wearing short skirts or shorts and should cover their heads with a scarf.

Pointing with the forefinger, pointing your feet at a person or touching a person's head is considered rude.

Taxi stand

PERHENTIAN TEKSI

Taxis

Kuala Lumpur is well served by a system of highways which bring commuters, taxis, buses and cars into the centre of the city. While traffic jams have not yet reached Bangkok's disastrous gridlocks, they are well on the way.

Underground tunnel at railway station

MONEY MATTERS

The Malaysian dollar is the ringgit (abbreviated to RM), which is worth 100 sen. Bank notes come in several denominations: RM2 (purple), RM5 (green), RM10 (red), RM20 (brownish-orange), RM50 (bluish-green), and RM100. Coins come in denominations of RM1 and 50, 20, 10, 5 and 1 sen.

Aside from everyday usage, coins are specifically needed for public phones (at 10 sen per local call), driver-operated ticket dispensers in public buses and vending machines for train and monorail tickets.

The ringgit was fixed at RM3.80 to US$1 at press time. Due to currency control regulations imposed in 1998, the ringgit cannot be traded outside the country.

Money changers can be found all over the city. Although rates vary, they offer better exchange rates than banks.

Traveller's cheques are accepted at major hotels, restaurants and department stores, although banks will give you the best rates.

Credit cards such as American Express, Diners Club, MasterCard and Visa are widely accepted by most establishments throughout Kuala Lumpur. Note that retail shops may impose a 2–5 percent surcharge if you pay for your shopping by credit card.

Tipping

Large service establishments such as hotels, restaurants, bars and clubs add a service charge automatically to bills, so tipping is not necessary. However, where where good service is rendered, a small tip will be appreciated. Taxis generally expect the exact meter fare.

Kuala Lumpur's taxis are conspicuously painted yellow and black or red and white. They offer a convenient and economical means of moving around the city, and drivers usually speak at least a smattering of English. Taxi drivers are proud of their credibility and occasionally make headlines with acts of honesty. Once befriended, they can make charming conversationalists and good sources of information.

Air-conditioning and fare meters are compulsory in all taxis. Make sure the meter is activated only after you get in. Rates are RM2 for the first 2 km (1.24 miles) and 10 sen for each additional 200 metres (half a mile). There is a surcharge of RM1 for calling for a cab by phone. There is also a 50 percent surcharge on the meter fare between midnight and 6am. If there are more than two passengers per taxi, 20 sen per ad-

Moorish arches

ditional passenger is levied. Hourly rates vary, some charge RM15 per hour, others add RM10 to the meter. City taxis cannot legally pick passengers up at the airport.

It is fairly easy to get a taxi either by queueing at taxi stands, flagging one down by the street, or booking one by telephone. Try to avoid hailing one between 3 and 3.30pm, as cab drivers change shifts around this time and usually do not pick up passengers unless you are going their way. Note: It will also be difficult to get a taxi in heavily jammed areas during rush hours.

Taxi coupons at fixed rates are available on arrival at the Kuala Lumpur International Airport. These coupons are necessary in order to take an airport limousine to the city or suburbs, and should be handed to the driver at the start of journey. The same system applies at the rail station, where tickets are sold near Platform 4.

Buses

There are several buses to choose from in Kuala Lumpur. City bus companies include Sri Jaya, Len Seng, Len Foh Hup, Toong Foong and Intrakota (air-conditioned). Air-con buses are 50 sen for the first 2 km and then 5 sen per km.

The main inner city bus stops are Puduraya, the Klang Bus Station near Chinatown, Bangkok Bank behind Central Market, Lebuh Ampang, and the Jalan Tuanku Abdul Rahman/Jalan Ipoh intersection in Chow Kit. Buses can be can-of-sardine proportions during peak periods, so watch your wallets.

Rental Cars

For seeing the city in style, opt for a chauffered limousine offered by a number of local car-rental companies, includng Avis, Budget, Hertz and National. Most hotels also provide air-conditioned limo services, but they tend to be more expensive.

For self-drive cars, rental rates vary according to insurance options and type of vehicle, so it is best to call around and enquire first.

Train and Light Rail

KTM Berhad also administers the Rawang to Klang KTM Komuter electrified commuter rail service, which transports commuters and travellers within greater Kuala Lumpur and the Klang Valley.

Within the city, the Light Rail Transport (LRT) is an integrated monorail system operated by two concessionaires, Putra and Star. The LRT services areas such as Jalan Ampang, Chow Kit, Petaling Jaya, and Bangsar. Feeder buses go to suburbs and shopping centres. Ask for maps at any station.

Maps

Tourism Malaysia (tel: 293 5188) has several free maps and guides covering various aspects of the city available from its information counters and in most hotels. The maps show routes, landmarks and commuter train and LRT stops within the city.

You can also get maps and more information from the Malaysian Tourist Information Complex (MATIC) at 109 Jalan Ampang. Tel: 264 3929.

HOURS AND HOLIDAYS
Business Hours

Business hours are 8.30am or 9am to 5pm, Monday to Friday. Many businesses are also open on Saturdays from 8.30 or 9am, closing by 12.30pm or 1pm. Government offices are open from 8am–4.15pm Monday through Friday, and from 8am–12.45pm on Saturday.

Banks are open 10am–3pm Monday to Friday, and 9.30am–11.30pm on Saturday. Post offices open from 8am–4.30pm, Monday to Saturday. The General Post Office at Menara Dayabumi, Jalan Sultan Hishamuddin has longer opening hours. The first Saturday of the month is a government and banking off-day. Hotels will mail letters and sell stamps at the reception desk. Almost all department stores, supermarkets and shopping complexes are open daily from 10am–10pm. Otherwise, shops close earlier, between 6.30–7.30pm and on Sunday.

Public Holidays

Following are official public holidays in Kuala Lumpur. Dates of ethnic festivals vary, they are determined by various lunar calendars. Check precise dates with Tourism Malaysia:

New Year's Day: January 1
Federal Territory Day: February 1
Chinese New Year: January/February
Hari Raya Puasa: Date varies
Labour Day: May 1
Wesak Day: May/June
HM the King's Birthday: June 5
Hari Raya Haji: Date varies
National Day: August 31
Prophet Muhammad's Birthday: Date varies
Deepavali: October/November
Christmas Day: December 25

ACCOMMODATION

Hotels

There is a current boom in hotel construction with several international-class names under construction. Hotels are all air-conditioned and complemented by restaurants and bars. Five-star hotels have swimming pools, fitness centres, shops and other facilities. Rack rates for standard double rooms are divided into five approximate price ranges: $=below RM100, $$=RM100–RM199 $$$=RM200–RM299 $$$$=RM300–RM399 $$$$$=above RM400;

APOLLO
106 Jalan Bukit Bintang
Tel: 242 8133
Close to shopping malls. $

CARCOSA SERI NEGARA
Taman Tasik Perdana

Tel: 282 1888
Immaculate suite hotel in a former Governor-General's residence and set in a private park. $$$$$

CHAMTAN HOTEL
62 Jalan Masjid India
Tel: 293 0144
Surrounded by excellent shopping, though entertainment is limited. $

CITY HOTEL
366 Jalan Raja Laut
Tel: 441 4466
A reasonably-priced establishment near the Chow Kit area. $

CONCORDE
2 Jalan Sultan Ismail
Tel: 244 2200
Not far from the shopping district and houses the Hard Rock Cafe. $$$

CROWN PRINCESS
Jalan Tun Razak
Tel: 262 5522
A well-appointed hotel, located next to major shopping malls. $$$

EQUATORIAL
Jalan Sultan Ismail
Tel: 261 7777
Located in the business district near shops and entertainment. $$$

FEDERAL
35 Jalan Bukit Bintang
Tel: 248 9166
One of KL's original hotels in the heart of Bukit Bintang. It has a revolving restaurant. $$$

FORTUNA
87 Jalan Berangan
Tel: 241 9111
Small but central; in a quiet area behind the main Bukit Bintang area. $$

GRAND CENTRAL
63 Jalan Putra
Tel: 441 3011
Close to the Putra World Trade Centre and The Mall. $$

The Railway Administrative Building

GRAND CONTINENTAL
Jalan Raja Laut
Tel: 293 9333
Located near the Jalan Tuanku Abdul Rahman shopping area. $$

HOTEL NIKKO KUALA LUMPUR
165 Jalan Ampang
Tel: 261 1111
Hotel with clean Japanese lines, close to the new KL City Centre. $$$$

ISTANA
Jalan Raja Chulan
Tel: 241 9988
A large hotel, centrally located to business and shops. $$$

JW MARRIOTT
Star Hill Centre, 181 Jalan Bukit Bintang
Tel: 291 8584
Quietly sophisticated hotel, close to all the major shopping centres. $$$$

KUALA LUMPUR HILTON
Jalan Sultan Ismail
Tel: 248 2322
Recently refurbished and well-known for its dance club, TM2. $$$$

KUALA LUMPUR PARKROYAL
54 Jalan Sultan Ismail
Tel: 242 5588
A well-located property in the heart of the shopping district. $$$$

MALAYA
Jalan Hang Lekir
Tel: 232 7722
In central Chinatown, surrounded by lots of shopping areas. $$

MALAYSIA
67–69 Jalan Bukit Bintang
Tel: 242 8033
A medium-class hotel along Jalan Bukit Bintang. $$

MANDARIN
2 Jalan Sultan
Tel: 230 3000
Also in the heart of Chinatown, close to major bus and taxi terminals and the Central Market cultural centre. $$

MANDARIN ORIENTAL
Kuala Lumpur City Centre
Tel: 380 8888
Luxury accommodation next to the world's tallest twin buildings. $$$$$

MELIA KUALA LUMPUR
16 Jalan Imbi
Tel: 242 8333
A short distance from the entertainment hub of Bukit Bintang. $$$$

MICASA HOTEL APARTMENTS
368B Jalan Tun Razak
Tel: 261 8833
The city's first all-suite hotel. Rooms have equipped kitchenettes. $$$$$

MING COURT VISTA HOTEL
Lot 2, Section 43
Jalan Ampang
Tel: 261 8888
A comfortable hotel catering to a largely business traveller clientele. $$$$

PAN PACIFIC
Jalan Putra
Tel: 442 5555
Good location; near the Putra World Trade Centre and The Mall. $$$$

PLAZA
Jalan Raja Laut
Tel: 298 2255
Close to the Chow Kit shops. $$

RENNAISANCE HOTEL/NEW WORLD HOTEL
Cnr Jalan Sultan Ismail/Jalan Ampang
Tel: 262 2233/263 6888
European-themed business hotel pair at the tip of the Golden Triangle. $$$$$/$$$$

SHANGRI-LA
11 Jalan Sultan Ismail
Tel: 232 2388
Centrally located in the business district and famed for its cuisine. $$$$$

SWISS INN
Jalan Sultan
Tel: 03-232 3333
Popular hotel in the heart of Chinatown with good people-watching sidewalk cafe. $$

THE LEGEND
Jalan Putra
Tel: 442 9888
Located next to the Mall and opposite the Putra World Trade Centre. $$$$

THE REGENT KUALA LUMPUR
160 Jalan Bukit Bintang
Tel: 241 8000
A polished establishment with excellent service and restaurants. $$$$$

Youth Hostels

KL INTERNATIONAL YOUTH HOSTEL
Jalan Kampung Attap
Tel: 273 6870
Within walking distance of Chinatown and major bus terminals. $

YMCA
95 Jalan Padang, Brickfields
Tel: 274 1439

Near the town centre, easily accessible by public transport. Has a gym as well as other sports facilities. $

Guest Houses

Many small hotels housed above shop units can be found in the city, especially along Jalan Tuanku Abdul Rahman and in the Chow Kit and Bukit Bintang areas. Better known by their old Malay name, *rumah tumpangan* (which means lodging houses), some of them are quite reputable. For example, the Merdeka Hotel in Jalan Raja Muda offers decent and clean rooms at prices lower than those of budget hotels. Room rates range from RM$40–55.

HEALTH AND EMERGENCIES

Hygiene

Tap water is safe to drink. Those unfortunate enough to have experienced that scourge of travellers – variously referred to as Delhi belly, Cairo curd or Montezuma's revenge – will be relieved to know Malaysian piped water is treated and unlikely to cause stomach upsets. Restaurants and other eating establishments offer boiled water. Mineral and bottled water is also widely available.

Food served in licensed restaurants and at hawker stalls is mostly clean. Regular customers are very important for hawker stalls so most try and keep their stalls and utensils clean.

Should problems arise, pharmacies are found in most shopping complexes. They are well-stocked and have registered pharmacists to attend to customers' needs. Controlled drugs are sold only by prescription.

Hospitals

Many hotels have doctors on call to treat emergencies. Kuala Lumpur has a number of hospitals offering good medical care. Both government and private hospitals have fully-equipped emergency and intensive care units to cope with any medical crisis.

The **General Hospital** is at Jalan Pahang, tel: 292 1044, and the **Universiti Hospital** is at Jalan Universiti in subur-

Local and international magazines are available at newsstands

ban Petaling Jaya, its emergency tel: 756 4422 ext 2500. They are both government-owned hospitals.

Private hospitals include: **Tawakal Specialist Centre**, 202-A Jalan Pahang, tel: 423 3599: **CMH Medical Centre**, 106 Jalan Pudu, tel: 238 2055; **Pantai Medical Centre**, 8 Jalan Bukit Pantai, tel: 282 5077; **Subang Medical Centre**, 1 Jalan SS12/1A Subang Jaya, tel: 734 1212.

Medical and Dental Clinics

There are many 24-hour polyclinics, or the privately-owned specialist clinics, which offer treatment in the city. Registered medical practitioners and qualified dental surgeons are listed in the Yellow Pages of the telephone directory.

Police Emergencies

The emergency number for police is 999, ambulance is 911 and fire is 994.

Emergency Repairs

Sidewalk cobblers and key grinders are found on almost every other downtown street and in shopping complexes. They do a pretty good job at fairly low prices. Some of them also make rubber stamps, signs, engravings and so on.

COMMUNICATIONS AND NEWS

Telecommunications

Telephone, telegram, mail, telex and fax facilities are offered by most hotels, and in the case of medium-budget to luxury hotels, IDD (international direct dial) phones are available in guest rooms. To call abroad directly, first dial the international access code 00, followed by the country code: Australia (61); France (33); Germany (49); Italy (39); Japan (81); Netherlands (31); Spain (34); UK (441); US and Canada (1).

To call Kuala Lumpur from overseas, dial the international country code 60 for Malaysia, followed by 3, the area code for Kuala Lumpur.

International calls can also be made at any Kedai Telekom (Telecoms shops) located in the city during office hours. A 24-hour service is available at the Central Telekom Building in Jalan Raja Chulan. IDD pay phones are also available in popular locations. They accept most major credit cards.

The cost of a local call through a public payphone is 10 sen. Payhones maintained at shops and restaurants charge twice or three times that amount. Calls may also be made using pre-paid phone cards. These cards, sold in denominations of RM5, RM10 and RM20, are very convenient and can be purchased at selected stores such as 7-Eleven and news sellers. Payphones using these phone cards are usually in better working order since they are less prone to vandalism.

Note, however, that payphones are maintained by three companies, Uniphone, Citiphone and

Telekom Malaysia, and that the various phone cards are not interchangeable.

Internet cafes are found everywhere, particularly in shopping centres, and charges range from RM4–10 per hour.

Shipping

Larger shops will handle documentation and shipping for purchases, or will recommend handling agents to do the job.

Stationery shops and some post offices sell boxes for goods to be sent by mail.

News Media

There are several English dailies in Peninsular Malaysia: *The Star* and *The Sun* (morning tabloids), *The New Straits Times* (morning broadsheet), *Business Times* and *Malay Mail* (afternoon tabloid). The two largest selling, *The Star* and *The New Straits Times*, offer comprehensive coverage of local and foreign news. The *Asian Wall Street Journal, International Herald Tribune* and *USA Today* can be obtained at most newsstands and bookshops. Some shops also offer newspapers such as the *Daily Mirror* and *The Times* from England, and dailies from the United States, Australia, Bangkok, Tokyo and other parts of the world. Leading international periodicals are available at large bookshops and hotel news sellers.

Radio Ibu Kota (Voice of the Capital City) is a 24-hour special service for Kuala Lumpur and has programmes for visitors and travellers. It is broadcast by the government-owned Radio Television Malaysia on 97.2 MHz. FM radio has a range of English-language musical programmes from classical to jazz and pop. RTM also broadcasts an English service, Radio Four Network, that begins at 6am daily and ends at midnight. English-language news bulletins are broadcast hourly. Flip through the stations and you will hear everything from canto-pop to Hindi movie film hits and Malay rock tunes.

SPORTS

Swimming

Almost all hotels charging RM200 and

above have swimming pools; those above RM300 also have health clubs, tennis and squash courts.

Public pools at **Bangsar Sports Complex** (tel: 282 4084); **Chin Woo Stadium** (tel: 232 4602); **Club Syabas** (tel: 757 3322); are open from 8am to midnight.

In addition, there is a massive water theme park in Bandar Sunway called **Sunway Lagoon** (tel: 735 6000). It is open from noon to 9pm.

Jogging

Taman Tasik Perdana (Lake Gardens), **Taman Tasik Titiwangsa** off Jalan Tun Razak, **Taman Tasik Permaisuri** in Cheras, **Taman Tunku Abdul Rahman**, and the KLCC **Park** have jogging paths.

Gym and Fitness Centres

Many hotels have fully-equipped fitness centres or gyms. Also try the Weld, Wisma HLA and PJ Hilton.

Court and Racquet Games

Sports complexes in and around the city offer facilities for badminton, tennis, squash, volleyball, table tennis and *sepak takraw* (a local ball game). Courts are open from 7 or 8am till 11pm or midnight: **Bangsar Sports Complex** (tel: 282 4084); **Kampung Datuk Keramat** (tel: 456 4853); **Taman Tasik Titiwangsa** (tel: 423 9558); **Bandar Tun Razak Sports Complex** (tel: 930 8935); and **National Sports Council Complex** (tel: 958 1390).

Bowling

Bowling alleys can be found at: **Federal Hotel**, Jalan Bukit Bintang, **Wisma Mirama** on the 5th floor and **Yow Chuan Plaza**, Jalan Tun Razak.

Golf

Malaysia is often called a golfer's paradise. There are hundreds golf courses in the country, some of them designed by luminaries like Ronald Fream, Jack Nicklaus and Robert Trent Jones. There are over fifty courses alone within an hour's drive from Kuala Lumpur. Some of these courses also offer night golfing under floodlights.

Close to the city is the famed **Royal Selangor Golf Club** (tel: 984 8433) off Jalan Tun Razak. Also fairly close to the city is the **Saujana Golf and Country Club** (tel: 746 1466) located near the Subang Airport, with a 36-hole golf course. Other clubs in the vicinity include the **Sultan Salahuddin Golf Club** (tel: 550 5872), **Glenmarie Golf and Country Club** (tel: 703 9090), both in Shah Alam. The Sultan Salahuddin also offers facilities for night golfing as well.

Further from KL is the **Rahman Putra Golf and Country Club** in Sungai Buluh (tel: 656 6870); **Templer Golf and Country Club** in Rawang (tel: 691 9617); **Awana Golf Club** in Genting Highlands (tel: 211 3015); and **Morib Golf Club** (tel: 858 1732).

Most clubs charge green fees for non-members. Further details may be obtained from the Malaysian Golfing Association, 12A, Persiaran Ampang, tel: 457 7931.

LANGUAGE

The Malay language, or Bahasa Malaysia, is polysyllabic, with variations in syllables to convey changes in meaning, unlike tonal languages such as Mandarin, Cantonese and Thai. For example, *duduk* (sit) is a verb. By adding the prefix *ke* and suffix *an*, we get the noun *kedudukan*, which means position. By adding a different prefix, *pen*, we get another noun, *penduduk*, which means inhabitant. Adding an *i* after *duduk* turns it into an active verb (to sit), while *menduduki* is a present continuous verb.

Tones do not vary to give different meanings and, for the most part, words are pronounced as they are spelt. In general, the pronunciation is the same as in English, with a few exceptions.

In Bahasa Malaysia, 'a' is pronounced 'ar' as in tar. The letter 'e' has an 'er' sound, as in reserve. You will also find that 'c' is pronounced 'ch' as in chair; the letter 'g' is always hard, as in gun and garden, not as in ginger; and 'sy' is pronounced 'sh'.

The language uses two distinct scripts: *Jawi* and *Rumi*. Jawi is the Arabic form of writing; *Rumi* the Roman alphabet, considered the easier of the two and also the official script of the country.

Here is a small vocabulary to get you on your way.

Numbers

1	*Satu*
2	*Dua*
3	*Tiga*
4	*Empat*
5	*Lima*
6	*Enam*
7	*Tujuh*
8	*Lapan*
9	*Sembilan*
10	*Sepuluh*
11	*Sebelas*
12	*Dua belas*
13	*Tiga belas*
20	*Dua puluh*

21	Dua puluh satu
100	Seratus
1,000	Seribu

Greetings and Others

How do you do?	Apa khabar?
Good morning	Selamat pagi
Good afternoon	Selamat petang
Good evening	Selamat malam
Goodbye	Selamat tinggal
Bon voyage	Selamat jalan
Fine/good	Baik
Thank you	Terima kasih
Please	Tolong/sila
Excuse me	Maafkan saya
I am sorry	Saya minta maaf
Yes	Ya
No	Tidak

Pronouns

I	Saya
You	Anda/awak
He/she	Dia
We	Kami
They	Mereka

Forms of Address

Mr	Encik
Mrs	Puan
Miss	Cik

Directions and Travel

Where	Di mana
Right	Kanan
Left	Kiri
Turn	Belok
Go	Pergi
Stop	Berhenti
Follow	Ikut
Near	Dekat

Far	Jauh
Inside	Dalam
Outside	Luar
Front	Hadapan
Behind	Belakang
Here	Sini
There	Sana
Road	Jalan
Street	Jalan
Lane	Lorong
Bridge	Jambatan
Junction	Simpang
North	Utara
South	Selatan
East	Timur
West	Barat

Useful Phrases

How much?	Berapa harganya?
Can you help me?	Bolehkah encik tolong saya?
Where is this place?	Di mana tempat ini?
How far?	Berapa jauh?
I want to go to…	Saya hendak pergi ke…
Stop here	Tolong berhenti sini
Expensive	Mahal
Lower the price	Kurangkan harganya
Too big	Besar sangat
Too small	Kecil sangat
Any other colour?	Ada warna lain?

Other Handy Words

Drink	Minum (verb), Minuman (noun)
Eat	Makan (verb), Makanan (noun)
Fruit	Buah-buahan
Water	Air
Have	Ada
Don't have	Tidak ada
Toilet	Tandas
Why?	Mengapa?
When?	Bila?
Hot (spicy)	Pedas
Hot (heat)	Panas
Cold	Sejuk
Sweet	Manis
Sour	Masam
Delicious	Sedap
Clean	Bersih

Dirty	*Kotor*
Beautiful	*Cantik*
Open	*Buka*
Close	*Tutup*
Never	*Tidak pernah*
Often	*Selalu*
Sometimes	*Kadang-kadang*

USEFUL ADDRESSES

Tourist Offices

TOURISM MALAYSIA
Level 2, 24–27th and 30th Floor
Putra World Trade Centre
Jalan Tun Ismail
Tel: 293 5188

MALAYSIA TOURIST INFORMATION
COMPLEX (MATIC)
109 Jalan Ampang
Tel: 264 3929
MATIC staff are knowledgeable and extremely helpful with tourist enquiries.

Tourism Malaysia Information Centres are also found at: Dataran Merdeka (underground), tel: 293 6664; Kuala Lumpur Railway Station, tel: 274 6063, KLIA (Arrival Hall), tel: 8787 4212.

Credit Card Offices

AMERICAN EXPRESS
5th Floor, Bangunan MAS
Jalan Sultan Ismail
Tel: 261 0000, 261 3000.
Hours: 8.30am–6pm Monday–Friday; 8.30am–noon Saturday

DINER'S CLUB
Wisma Tan and Tan, Jalan Tun Razak.
Tel: 261 1322, 261 1055.
Hours: 9am–5pm Monday–Friday; 9am–1pm Saturday

MBF MASTERCARD SERVICES
12th floor, Wisma MCA, Jalan Ampang.
Tel: 262 2222.
Hours: 9am–5pm Monday–Friday; 9am–1pm Saturday

FURTHER READING

Most bookshops carry a mediocre range of titles, with perhaps the exceptions being the University of Malaya's bookshop and Skoobs in Brickfields.

Major bookstores include the Berita Book Centre in Bukit Bintang Plaza, Times Distributors with branches in Sungei Wang Plaza and the Weld, MPH in Bangsar and Jaya's, Petaling Jaya, as well as Popular bookstores in Atrium and Jalan Petaling. The titles listed here are only a selection of the publications available in Malaysia.

The Malayan Trilogy, Burgess, Anthony. London: Penguin Books. Burgess' famous novel on post-war Malaya during the chaotic upheaval of independence.

Culture Shock! Malaysia and Singapore, Craig, Jo-Ann. Times Books Intl. Interesting notes on the country's customs.

Turtle Beach, d'Alpuget, Blanche. Penguin 1981. Award-winning Australian novel on the plight of the Vietnamese people and their arrival in Malaysia.

The Malay Archipelago, Wallace, Alfred Russell. Singapore: Graham Brash, 1987. Wallace's famous account of his travels in the region. During his time in the East, Wallace formulated the theory of natural evolution, only to find that his contemporary Darwin had beaten him to the press.

The Malays – A Cultural History, Winstedt, Richard. Revised and updated by Tham Seong Chee. Singapore: Graham Brash, 1981. A fascinating documentation of the Malay people from pre-history to the present day.

Adoi by Lee Kit. Times Books International, Singapore/Kuala Lumpur, 1989. A humourous, well-illustrated satire of Malaysian foibles and fancies.

Chinatown, Kuala Lumpur by Bristow, Steve and Lee, Edwin. Tropical Press, KL, 1994. Excellent photographs and history of the city's Chinatown.

Insight Guide Malaysia. Apa Publications, 1999. Best-selling book retains the basic structure of the original book published in 1985, with scores of new photographs and updated text.

Index